中国历史纲要

Special thanks to Houghton Mifflin
Company, Boston for use of certain
maps in English contained herein
and derived from EAST ASIA: The Mod-
dern Transformation, by John K. Fairbank, Edwin O. Reischauer and Albert
M. Craig.

ISBN: 978-0-88710-091-8

Contents

中国历史纲要目次

Maps, Charts, and Tables

The Yale   For a long time the process of developing a
'Mirror   series of texts has been going on at Yale
Series'   University. Texts used at the Institute of
            Far Eastern Languages, known as the 'Mirror
Series', include the following for spoken Chinese:

     SPEAK CHINESE, by M. Gardner Tewksbury, a beginner's
         text based on the structural patterns of
         spoken Mandarin and the grammatical princi-
         ples to be found in them. (Vocabulary 600)

     CHINESE DIALOGUES, by Fred Wang, dialogs based on
         vocabularies of everyday life. This is
         planned to follow *Speak Chinese* as a second
         level text. (Vocabulary 1000)

and the following for written Chinese:

     READ CHINESE BOOKS One, Two and Three. Introduce
         1000 characters and their simplified equiva-
         lents (approximate total 1300). Texts in
         vernacular Chinese, fully coordinated with
         the spoken texts.

     READINGS ON CHINESE CULTURE, IFEL Staff. Twelve
         lessons on various aspects of Chinese culture
         and politics meant as a review text for the
         three readers. Minimum introduction of new
         vocabulary.

For use of the present work the student is advised to
complete the two spoken texts, and at least the three
readers. Many other supplementary aids are also available for reinforcement at the various levels. Tapes for
all the books (including this text) are available and
recommended for use.

Historical Zhōngguo Lìshĭ Gāngyào, as the name applies,
Vocabulary is a very sketchy summary of Chinese History
            from earliest times down to the establishment
of the first republic in 1912. Its primary object is to
familiarize the student with the terms and patterns used

in discussing current affairs. Secondarily and inci-
dentally it gives him a few of the basic facts of
Chinese history and culture. In actual use, it has been
found to be a good preparation for Newspaper Chinese.
The style is a mixture of *báihùa* and what has been
termed *báihùawén*. Thus it provides a transition from
the pure vernacular to the modern language of print.
Needless to say, it provides a good general vocabulary
for classroom discussion of current political, social
and economic questions.

Classroom procedure based on this text will necessarily differ with the teacher. It may not be out of place, however, to enumerate here some of the practices which have been used both at the Institute of Far Eastern Languages at Yale University, and at the College of Chinese Studies in Peking. Following the text, two types of teaching aids are included: English sentences for translation into Chinese, and oral report topics.

Sound   Since this textbook aims at fluency in the
Recordings   spoken language, the lesson should be intro-
                duced orally rather than visually. If the
instructor can give this oral introduction by reading the chapter interpretively to the class, that is probably the ideal approach. He can interject explanations of new terms in Chinese, thus giving an exercise in comprehension at the same time that he introduces the lesson materials. Whether this is feasible or not, the student should listen to a sound recording before he even looks at the text. A second listening to the record may be followed with textbook open. Starting with the sound record, even before the vocabulary has been studied, means that every new term is first met *in its proper setting* rather than in isolation. In a large proportion of cases, it will be found that a new term may be guessed from its use in a setting. If this experience comes first, the study of the vocabulary is made easier, less time-consuming, and more effective.

A recent class was asked toward the end of their course whether they felt that the final edition of this text should include a glossary. They unanimously rejected the idea as unnecessary in the light of their experience. They had learned to guess many new words from the context.

Question   The traditional question and answer drill is
and Answer   a method which cannot safely be slighted, not
                to say superseded. Drills should be in small
groups, ideally of not more than five students. Questions should be asked at the speed of normal speech and the aim should be to get prompt as well as idiomatic

answers. If the answer is not promptly forthcoming, it
is probably that the instructor's question was too
advanced for the student. Many simple questions accomplish more than a few complicated ones. Questions for
classroom use prepared in advance by the teacher should
be of increasing difficulty. It has been found that
after ten or a dozen sessions of direct questions, simple topics may be assigned for oral report or paragraph
length. Toward the end of the text, topics have been
assigned which require a little reading in some English
text on Chinese history in preparation for a 10 minute
report in Chinese.

Memorization Instructors differ as to how much memory
                work should be required but agree that
some of it is essential. It helps the student to
acquire long phrases and sentences which can be tossed
off at high speed and thereby increase fluency. It
seems appropriate to require the memorization of a
selected paragraph here and there throughout the text.
The colloquial renderings from classical writers found
in Chapter 5 lend themselves to such use; likewise the
stories of Chapter 11. A longer story for memorization
has been prepared in connection with Chapter 21, and is
printed following the sentences for translation.

Translation Rendering the Chinese text into English
               has been found a rather futile procedure
and wasteful of both teacher and student time. It is
customary to allow time for the student to ask for
explanation of passages which he has not been able to
work out. The instructor does this explaining in
Chinese as far as possible, resorting to English only
where absolutely necessary. Adequate question drills
will insure that the student has mastered the content
of the chapter. The real need is for carefully checked
translation from English to Chinese. For this purpose
a set of sentences or paragraphs has been prepared for
each chapter. These likewise have been graduated from
the level of sentences which can be turned into Chinese
more or less word for word to that ultimate level on
which the translator has to ask himself not 'How does

that word translate into Chinese?' but 'How would Chinese express that thought?' The student soon learns that the lengthy sentences characteristic of English writing frequently have to be broken down into several sentences in Chinese, and that the word order may need to be completely changed.

It has been our practice to have the student bring to class a written translation of these English sentences and correct his own work in the light of the instructor's blackboard discussion of the several possible ways to translate each sentence. Thus the sentences are treated as practice work rather than as a test to be graded. Written and oral examinations are given at stated intervals.

Vocabulary The number of new terms involved in this text is rather heavy, running to about 1000 in all. Of these, a considerable number are combinations in which one or more elements are already familiar. To encourage acquisition of new terms by the analysis-synthesis method, these semi-new items are grouped under major items in the general vocabulary.

It is my considered judgment that it is better to expose the student to a large vocabulary but not hold him responsible for the entire list, expecting him to retain those items which frequently recur, than to give him a limited vocabulary and expect him to retain every item.

Time should be reserved, after the class has studied a given assignment for questions on the new terms and their usage. The instructor should offer examples of the different uses of a given item appropriate to the lesson.

Maps and Charts The first tentative version of this text had no graphic aids. It soon became apparent that simplified maps could perform a double function, clarifying geographic situations referred to in the text, and at the same time offering something concrete to guide a student's recitation. Many a reci-

tation has since consisted largely of explaining a map
in Chinese. Similarly time charts have been used as out-
lines for unprepared oral reports in class. Any device
which gives the student a cue without giving him at the
same time the patterns of speech needed to follow the
cue has value in the classroom.

John S. Montanaro
General Editor, Mirror Series
1982

中国历史纲要

第一章　中国立国

序　言

　　你们大概学过美国历史，也许还看过世界历史，那么中美两国的历史有几个不同的地方，自然是知道的。例如：美国是一个新兴国家，没有五百年的历史，中国可不然，他立国的年代在四千年上下以前，就已经开始了。美国历史因为是近代的，所以有可靠的证据；中国历史，因为年代那么长，可就不同了。他头两千年的证据很少，就是有也不一定靠的住。

夏　代

　　美国人都知道美国是在一七七六年立的国，也许有人要问中国立国的年代一定是在前四千年吗？这个问题不容易回答。按着新历史家说，纪元前两千年，在黄河下流的两边已经有了中国人。他们的文化比较四周围民族的文化进步的多。那时候人民所用的器具还都是石头造的，因为铜铁还没发现呢，所以生活是很简单的。除去种一点小米，打鱼，打猎以外就是打仗。房子也不象现在的房子这么讲究。冬天住的房子是地里挖的坑，房顶是树枝做的。夏天天气一暖和了，人民就赶快的爬出坑来，

1

在树里盖房子，这是因为他们很怕野兽。那时候在中国北部已经有老虎，有野猪，也有象。

在铜器没发现以前，当然不能有铜钱，所以做买卖都是对换东西。有的东西是从很远的地方来的，例如：中亚洲跟南洋。在中国历史上这个时代就叫夏朝或是夏代。因为那时候山西省西南部有一个最开化的城，名叫夏。这个夏国的领土很小，只有山西省汾河流域的下部，可是这带地是中国文化的起源，也可以说是中国文化的发源地。

第二章 商 代

在纪元前一千七百来年，商国兴起来了。起头商国也就是一个大城，管理周围的些个村庄。领土也是在山西省的西南部，可是商国的文化比邻国的文化进步的多；所以邻国慢慢地受了商国的影响，到了儿也被他同化了。商朝的文化可不象夏朝的文化。夏朝是石器文化，商朝是铜器文化，用铜造器具。这是一种很大的进步。商朝人所造的铜器，到现在还是精美无比的。

还有一样的进步，就是夏朝人都是在地洞里住，或者在树上。商朝人不然；他们会造砖盖房子，当然就是有钱的人能用砖盖房，其余的老百姓还是住洞住树。吃食也还是简单的。肉类不过是猪，狗，鸡，鱼，这几样；粮食就是大米，小米，跟高粱。猪，狗，鸡都是在家里养活的。牛羊马这一类的大动物还是没有的。

安　阳

商朝的历史上有一件很要紧的事情。在纪元前一千四百年上下，京城还在山西省，离潼关不远。不知道是因为什么缘故，商朝决定把京城搬到东边儿去。也许是因为西北方的敌人太强盛，商朝打不过他们，就想要躲避他们的侵略。

无论怎么样，商朝迁都了，迁到现在河南省的北部。在这个新地方造了一个很大的城，名叫安阳，宫殿盖的又宽又大，城里的街修的又宽又直，以前中国人没看过那么美的一个城。商朝越来越兴旺，领土比夏朝的领土大的多，从现在的万里长城一直到淮河，从山东的泰山，一直到陕西的潼关。

过了四百年，安阳这个城被西北边来的一个周人毁了，商朝就灭亡了。　近来有考古学家把安阳城的根基给挖出来了，所以我们现在知道安阳有多大，并且从地里挖出来的有许多商朝的器具，有铜器也有石器，有军队用的武器，也有老百姓用的家伙。从这些证据可以看出来那时候人民的生活是什么样的。

文　字

现在不能决定中国字是什么时候发明的。也许在商朝以前，已经有了很简单的字。反正商朝那时候人很会写字，这是一定的。绸子，木头，竹片，铜器，骨头，都成了他们写字或刻字

用的东西了。绸子，木头，竹片，早就毁了；可是铜器和骨头还存在。带字的骨头，已经挖出来的有好几万块，那没挖出来的，恐怕还很多吧。

pieces

Kongpa

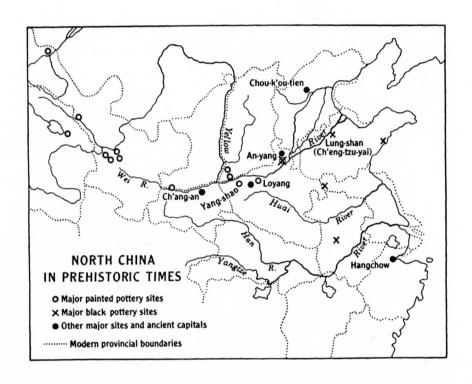

NORTH CHINA
IN PREHISTORIC TIMES

○ Major painted pottery sites
✕ Major black pottery sites
● Other major sites and ancient capitals
······ Modern provincial boundaries

第三章　周　朝

商朝的领土在黄河流域的下部，在黄河的中部——就是现在的陕西，甘肃两省——有些个半开化的民族，势力越来越大。到了纪元前第十一世纪当中，他们打败商朝，立了周朝。这些半开化的人怎么能胜过一个非常开化的国家呢？一个缘故是因为商朝国内有许多人起来反对，帮助周人来消灭商朝。

周朝的三个时代

周朝的京城是立在陕西的长安。在历史上周朝的年代最长。从纪元前一千零二十七年一直到二百二十一年，这八百年可分作三个时代。

西周时代⋯⋯⋯纪元前一○二七年——七七一年
东周时代⋯⋯⋯纪元前七七一年——四七四年
战国时代⋯⋯⋯纪元前四七四年——二二一年

在头二百五十年，周朝的几个王都是很有本事的人，所以周朝很强盛，领土发展到长江中部⋯⋯⋯就是现在的湖南省。到了第八世纪，周朝就衰弱了。那时候的王也不如以前的王了。在七百七十一年从西北边又来了些个半开化的人，打进长安，把周朝的王也杀了。周朝就迁都了，迁到东边河南省的洛邑⋯⋯⋯⋯就是现在的洛阳，因为京城从西边搬到东边去了，所以历史上管这个时代叫东周时代。洛邑比长安容易保守，可是从这

时候起，王的势力越来越小，各国的诸候都看不起王了，也不遵守他的命令了。

战国时代

从纪元前四百七十四年起，虽然周朝还是称王，可是实力一点也没有了。全国分作许多小国，都彼此相争。大国消灭小国，直到剩下七个国家。又过了几十年，才剩下两个大国。一个是西北边的秦国，一个是南边的楚国。最后秦国胜过楚国，就把全国都统一起来了。这是中国全国头一次真正的统一。秦王政不但统一了以前周朝的领土，并且打到南海。中国本部就有两个地方，他没打到；一个是云南贵州，两省的山地，一个是福建浙江两省沿海的地方。

文化的进步

这八百年，中国的文化，有很大的进步。商朝是铜器时代，周朝可以算是铁器时代。起头人看铁是很宝贵的，只用铁造武器。到了周朝末年，连农人耕地用的各种器具也是铁造的。商业也很发展。起头交易的方法是拿东西对换，后来就改用铜钱了。这古钱的样子绝对不象现在的毛钱铜子儿，也不象前几十年的小铜钱。有的是刀的形式，有的是钟的形势，还有许多别的种类，真可以说：五花八门。这时代中国人也得到三种的牲

口，对于通商很有关系，这就是驴，骡子，骆驼。中国人已经有了马，可是马为驮东西用，不大好，不老实。驴，骡子，骆驼，这三种牲口比马容易管。

周朝的文字是中国最宝贵的。中国书最古的要算是诗经。其中有几篇诗大概是第八世纪写的。现在所存在的文字多半都是属于哲学一方面的。下边我们还要多讲这种文字，所以现在不多说了。中国的建造，也有进步。一些小国都造了长城围着他们的领土，为的是防备别国侵占。有的国也造了运河，一面为的是运粮食，一面为的是用水浇灌田地。在黄河的流域也常闹水灾，所以人民造河堤防备洪水毁坏田地。可不单有水灾也有旱灾。有的国盖大仓房，年头好的时候，征收粮食存在仓房里，等到年头不好的时候，就有粮米可以放给人民。

现代中国文化的根基多半建立在周朝。

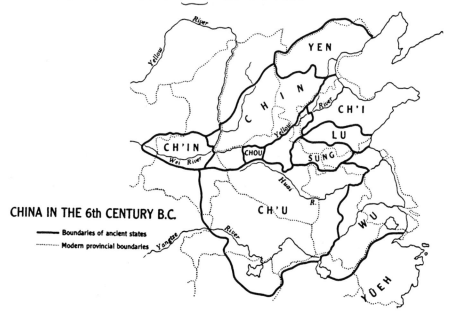

CHINA IN THE 6th CENTURY B.C.

—— Boundaries of ancient states
········· Modern provincial boundaries

第四章　周朝的哲学家

有的人一想到周朝，就不知不觉的想到孔子。人这么想，并没有什么奇怪，因为周朝对于中国文化最大的贡献，就是许多有名的哲学家。第一名当然是孔子。除了他以外，还有好几位有名的哲学家，都是在周朝的后半期出来的。这个时代也叫战国时代，因为几十个国家常常彼此相争。这样的内乱，对于人民的思想很有影响，就使人民想法子来解决社会上各样的难题。

儒　家

这些位大思想家之中，对于将来的中国最有影响的一位是孔子。他的名字是孔丘。他在纪元前五百来年作过鲁国的官他常想要改良社会。在他看，人性本来是好的，经过社会习俗的改变，才慢慢的坏了。孔子说要是国王跟官长都作好人，人民也就好了。国王要是不打仗不争地盘，人民也就不打架不偷东西了。孔子自己没作多少书。他的教训都是他的学生后来给记下来的。其中有一句最要紧的话是：「你不愿意人怎么样待你，你也不要怎么样待人」。孔子死了以后一百多年，有一位孟子作了一本书，讲明孔子的教训。孟子以后还有荀子，把孔子的教训作成了有系统的学说。后来的人就管孔子的学生叫儒家。他们大家的学说就叫儒学。

8

道家 Daoist

　　第二个大学派是道家。在孔子那时候有一位李耳，后来都称他老子。他也想要改变社会。他也看人性自然是好的，可是他说人民根本用不着政府跟法律来管理，自然就会做好事。有很多人喜欢他的思想。他死了以后几十年有一位庄子…………也叫庄周…………讲明他的道理。

墨家 ~ Moist

　　在孔子以后，还有一位墨翟（墨子）。他的学说最注重的是兼爱。兼爱的意思是我们不要只爱本家的人，也要爱世界上所有的人；所以墨子反对侵略，讲天下一家的道理。

法家 - fajia - Legalist

　　还有一种学派叫法家。他们的看法跟孔子老子的看法不同。在他们看，人性本来是不好的，得用法律来管，才能成好人。在第四世纪，有一位法家名叫商鞅，是秦国的大臣，帮助秦国的孝公改造他的国家。用了他们的方法实在能使秦国很强盛，打倒别的国家。过了一百年又出了两个法家韩非子跟李斯，帮助秦始皇建立统一的帝国。可惜韩非子没用就死了。李斯给他定了很重的法律为管理全国的人。

四个大学派

大多数的中国哲学家可以分作四个学派：儒家，道家，墨
家，法家。秦始皇不佩服儒家，喜欢道家。他烧的书多半是儒
家的书。可是汉朝的皇帝很佩服儒家，叫文人把古书都再写出
来了，所以孔子的教训，还能传到现在。到后来墨家渐渐的消
灭了。等到第十九世纪才有中国人注重他的学说。胡适博士说：
墨子的教训跟耶稣的教训有很多相同的地方。

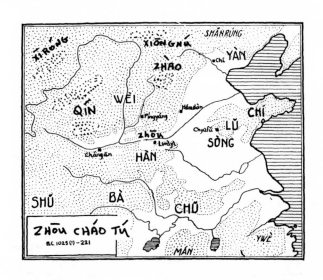

第五章　四个学派的教训

例 子 — Lizi — example

以下有几个例子，可以表明这每一家的教训。因为本文的文字，不容易看得懂，所以这些例子都翻出很简单的白话来了。

孔子的「大学」

古时候的人要向天下表明他的美德，

　　总是先管理他本国。

要管理他本国，

　　就先要管理他本家。

要管理他本家，

　　就先要管理他本人。

要管理他本国，

　　就先要管理他本家。

要管理他本家，

　　就先要管理他本人。

要管理他本人的思想，

　　就先要增加他的知识。

要增加他的知识，

　　就得研究各样的事情。

11

老子的「三件宝贝」

bao bei:
treasures

我有三件宝贝，
　是我很注意保存的：

baocun - preserve / protect

　　第一是：慈爱。 *ci'ai - love/humanity*

　　第二是：俭省。 *jiansheng - frugal*

　　第三是：不抢先。 *qiang xian - 0 do not be selfish or try to be first*

你要是「慈爱」

　　那么什么难事你都敢做了。

gan
boldly do

你要是「俭省」

　　那么就有敷余了。 *fuyu - create surplus*

你要是「不抢先」

　　就能得着领袖的地位。 *position*

leader

lingxiu

墨子的「兼爱」

怎么能叫人彼此相爱？

墨子说：

like/as
rutong

　　得看别人的国，如同自己的国一样。

　　得看别人的家，如同自己的家一样。

　　得看别人如同自己一样。

要是国王彼此相爱，就不能再打仗了。

要是家主彼此相爱，就不能再相争了。

jia wang

要是各人都彼此相爱，就不能再相害了。

要是父子彼此相爱，家里一定是有礼的。

要是兄弟彼此相爱，家里一定是和睦的。

要是世界上的人都彼此相爱，
　　强的就不欺负那弱的了。

　　人多的就不欺负那人少的了。

　　作官的就不小看平民了。

　　聪明的人就不欺骗那没有知识的人了。

每个人真要是「兼爱」这些坏事情就都不能有了。

韩非子注重法律

韩非子说：一个人有一个不好的儿子，竟做坏事：

　　他父母对他生气，他也不改；

　　村里的人都批评他，他也不改；

　　先生教训他，他也不改。

父母的爱心，人民的批评，先生的教训，都用尽了；

　　就是连他腿上的一根毛也没说动。

　　等到衙门里派人来拿他，他这才改。

　　可是要是没有法律，他是改不了的。

庄子的蝴蝶儿

大概各国的哲学家，都用过故事来表出他的思想。耶稣常用

这个法子，希腊国的名人，也是这样的。　在中国孔子，老子，孟子，墨子，也都用过。　可是最有意思的是庄子作的这个短故事。

　　庄子说：「有一次我庄周做了一个梦，梦见我是一个蝴蝶儿飞来飞去，很象是一个真蝴蝶儿。我只想那蝴蝶儿的快乐，不觉得我是庄周。过不大会儿我醒了，又是我自己了。现在我不知道是那时候人做梦变成了蝴蝶儿了哪，还是蝴蝶儿作梦变成人了哪！

中 国 哲 学 家 的 学 派

东
周
朝

第六世纪的思想生出
四个学派

500-

儒 家
孔 子

道 家
老 子

474

孔子的学生
子思
子路
曾子

墨 家
墨子

杨朱

400-

庄 子
讲明老子的
教训

战
国
时
代

法 家
是从内乱生
出来的

300-

孟 子
讲 明
孔子的教训

商 鞅

荀 子

墨 学
在第三世
纪灭亡

韩非子

221

200-

秦
朝

李 斯

205

儒 学

道 学

西
汉
朝

100-

15

第六章 秦朝统一中国

秦　朝　纪元前二二一至二〇七

我们讲战国时代的时候，已经提到秦国胜过楚国，就把中国本部都统一起来了。这位统一中国的国王名叫秦王政。他打了二十六年的仗（二四七至二二一）才成功。他做了皇帝，就给自己起了名字叫始皇帝，意思就是头一个皇帝。他很希望他的后人也可以作皇帝一直到万辈，可是他的儿子没有多大本事，大臣们就把他杀了，这是在二百〇七年。

以后有五年的内乱，以前的楚国又复兴起来了，差不多就要成功了，可是到了儿，有一位名誉不大的人刘邦，把楚王打的大败，就立了汉朝。

中央政治

周朝那时候老百姓不能自己买田地，田地都在贵族手里，农夫不过给他的主人耕田。　所收的粮米，一部分归主人，一部分归他们自己。　农夫不算主人的产业，可是也不能离开他所种的那块地，所以老百姓没有多大自由。　这叫封建制度。前八九百年，欧洲也有这样的封建制度。　秦始皇最大的贡献，就是消灭封建制度，给中国立一种中央政府。　他把全国分成三十六个省，派他可靠的人去作每一省的官长。那么样，地方

16

官就不常彼此相争，都得遵守皇帝的命令了。

法　律

秦朝以前，各国有各国的法律，这国的刑罚很重，那国的刑罚很轻，法律不一致。　秦始皇给全国定了一致的法律。人民可以知道什么是可作的，什么是不可作的。

万里长城

中国长久跟北边的一种鞑子打仗，名叫匈奴。在中国的北部，靠近匈奴住的地方，有许多小国家，已经造了大墙，为的是抵抗这些鞑子。秦始皇把这些短墙连起来了，作成一个很长的城墙，就是万里长城。现在还是在中国北边，西头在甘肃省，东头一直到渤海。长城到海岸的地方，叫山海关，因为在这个地方山离海不过有几里地。

别的工作

秦始皇还觉得中国的交通要不改良，就不容易管理他的四十一个省，也不容易运粮食，所以他就叫人造了一条大运河，也修了许多公路。

杀文人烧书

那个时候有许多文人，反对皇帝作的事情。这是因为皇帝

不照着周朝的方法，也不服从古人的教训。他有他自己计划来改造国家，所以皇帝杀了许多反对他的文人，也把很多古书给烧了。因为这个缘故，我们现在缺少可靠的周朝证据。

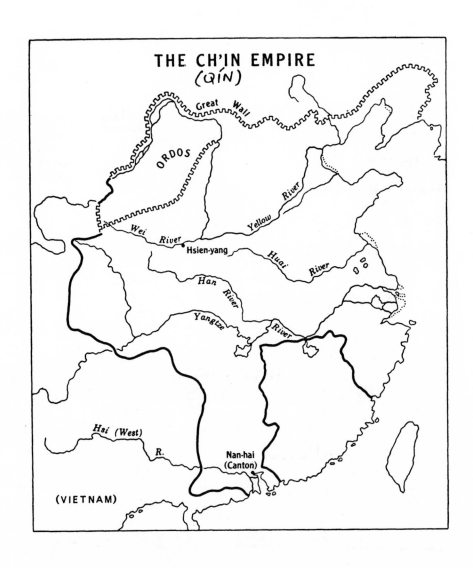

THE CH'IN EMPIRE
(QÍN)

第七章　汉朝

东西汉

汉朝是从纪元前二百〇六年到纪元后二百二十年，一共有四百二十二年的历史。在这四百多年的当中，我们可以把他分作前后两个时期。前期是从纪元前二百〇六年到纪元后二十五年。后期是从二十五年到二百二十年。前期汉朝的京城是在长安。后期汉朝的京城是在洛阳。因为长安是在西边，洛阳是在东边，所以历史上称汉朝的前期叫做前汉，又叫做西汉。称汉朝的后期叫做后汉，又叫做东汉。

西　汉

汉朝的头一个皇帝是刘邦，他是一个很能干的皇帝。在中国皇帝里头，从平民出身的他是第一个人。西汉时代汉朝有几个很有名的皇帝，最有名的是汉武帝。可是西汉的皇帝都有一个毛病。他们不相信大臣，也不相信自己家里的人。他们相信皇后家里的人。在纪元后第八年，有一个皇后家里的人，王莽，把刘家的皇帝推翻，自己做了皇帝。王莽这个人，有的人说他

19

坏。现在我们可以说他是中国一个政治改革家。他对于中国的
官制，田制，跟币制，都有极大的改革。可是在那个时代，他
的方法也许不很适用。王莽作了十五年皇帝。到了纪元后二十
三年，他的军队被刘家的军队打败了，他也被杀了。过了两年，
刘家的一位刘秀作了皇帝，慢慢的又把中国统一了。这个刘秀
就是东汉的头一个皇帝，光武帝。

东　汉

　　汉光武是一个爱百姓爱大臣的好皇帝。他以后的几个皇帝
也很好。他们开学校，学生最多的时候，有三万多人。可是后
来东汉的皇帝就软弱了。他们也有一个共同的毛病。他们不相
信大臣，也不相信家里的人，他们相信宦官。宦官是皇后宫里
的一种男佣人。在东汉灭亡以前的几十年，宦官的势力很大，
作了很多坏事。后来大臣们把宦官灭了，可是大家都看不起刘
家的皇帝了。谁有势力谁就是皇帝。你打我，我打你，闹了三
十来年。最后在二百二十年，汉朝被三国时代的魏国推翻，中
国全国分做魏国，蜀国，吴国，三个国家。

汉朝的国界

　　秦汉时代是中国很强的时代。秦朝的国界东边到海跟朝鲜，
西边到甘肃青海，南边到越南，北边到现在辽宁省的沈阳。汉

朝的国界比秦朝的国界大多了，东边到了朝鲜的汉江，南边到了交趾，西边到了帕米尔山，北边到了蒙古的沙漠。现在的中国人，也叫汉人，就是从那时候起的。中国的五族就是：汉，满，蒙，回，藏。汉武帝时代，他的一个大将有一次把匈奴一直打到贝加尔湖。在汉光武的末年，日本国派使臣到中国来进贡。在那个时候，汉朝管日本国叫倭奴国。「倭奴国」，这三个字，是小人国的意思。

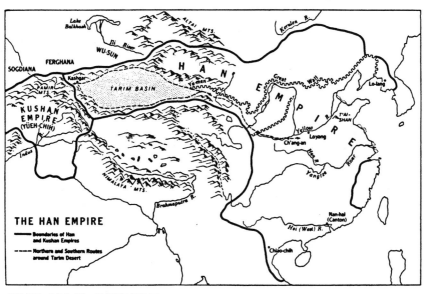

THE HAN EMPIRE

▬▬▬ **Boundaries of Han and Kushan Empires**

---- **Northern and Southern Routes around Tarim Desert**

第八章　汉朝通西域

汉武帝

汉朝最有名的皇帝是汉武帝。他的祖父高祖，已经把国内事情都治理好了。武帝的大难题，是北方的匈奴。秦始皇的万里长城挡不住他们，得想别的法子。武帝想起来西北方有一族人叫月氏，也受过匈奴的攻击。要是能得到他们的帮助，一同打匈奴，也许可以把鞑子赶出去，不再受他们的侵略。

张骞出使西域

所以他打发一位军官，名叫张骞，出使到月氏去，（氏读支）跟他们立条约。张骞带着一百个马兵，就往西北去。一出万里长城，就被匈奴拿住了。张骞没有法子，就假意归顺他们，他跟匈奴住了十年，娶了一个匈奴妻子，得了一个儿子，可是心里总想要达成武帝的目的。过了十年好容易得着一个机会，他就跟一个朋友逃跑了。他们一直的往西去找月氏。过了阿尔泰山，也过了天山，一共走了一万来里路，就找着了月氏国。三十七年以前，（纪元前一六五）匈奴把月氏赶出甘肃省的西北部，他们逃到帕米尔山西边的大夏国。这带地很肥，雨水多，也离匈奴远，所以他们就住下了。

22

张骞回国

张骞在月氏国，住了一年，常劝他们回去，帮助中国打匈奴，可是他们不肯受那么大的苦。过了一年他回中国的时候，又被匈奴拿住了。这次只跟他们住了一年。匈奴分争的时候，他又逃跑了，回到长安。这次把妻子，儿子，也带回来了。

张骞的报告

张骞报告皇帝的时候，他注重这几件事：一、虽然月氏不愿意回来，西北边还有别的国肯帮助中国打匈奴，中国应当跟他们联络。二、中亚洲有两条道路，一个北路，一个南路，南路离匈奴远一点儿。用南路通商，比北路平安。三、中亚洲的大宛国（宛读作元）有一种马，叫「天马」，比中国的马大的多。中国应当跟大宛国交易，得这种马。四、在大夏国，张骞在市场里看见方竹竿儿，不是本地长的，是从印度来的。中国东南部，四川，贵州，云南，三省，也出这种的方竹竿儿，所以按着张骞想的，印度一定是跟云南通过商。

报告的结果

这个报告有三个要紧的结果：

一、武帝派张骞回到中亚洲，跟些小国立条约。张骞也从大宛国带回「天马」来了，和几种中国以前所没有的出产。二、

武帝发兵去攻打南路和北路，把匈奴打败了。三、武帝又派张骞，到云南去找一个东南路，到印度，可是因为山高水大，道路很危险，张骞没通到印度。自从张骞这几次的旅行，中国才注意中亚洲。汉朝强的时候，这南北两路，都归中国管，后来弱了，也就管不了啦。

班超通西域

前汉通西域的有张骞。在后汉就是班超了。自从张骞的旅行以后，西域各国都作了中国的属国。到王莽的时候，西域各国造反，就跟匈奴联合起来独立了。到了东汉第二个皇帝时代，班超到西域去，叫各国来进贡。他第一次到西域去的时候只带着三十六个人。他走到一个国家，那国的国王心里想作中国的属国，可是匈奴派来的人劝他不要到中国进贡。国王不知道怎么办好。班超想了法子，他带着三十六个兵，夜里跑到匈奴住的地方，把匈奴派来的一百多人都杀了。国王看见班超有这么大的本事，害怕的了不得，就作了中国的属国了。以后班超又到西域去了好几次。那时候西域各国常常打仗，强国打弱国，大国打小国。班超只打强国大国，西域各国才平定下来。他在西域一共有三十一年。作中国属国的国家，一共有五十几个国。他到的地方比张骞还远。张骞只到了阿富汗。班超一直到了波斯。他还想到那时候的罗马帝国，到了波斯湾，他看波斯跟罗马正打仗哪，就回去了。东汉灭亡以前的几十年，罗马国的商人经过安南到中国来了一次。

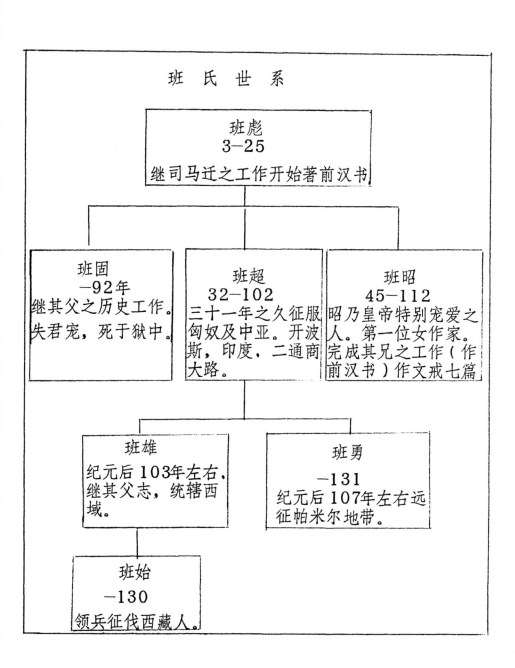

班 氏 世 系

班彪
3—25
继司马迁之工作开始著前汉书

班固
—92年
继其父之历史工作。失君宠，死于狱中。

班超
32—102
三十一年之久征服匈奴及中亚。开波斯，印度，二通商大路。

班昭
45—112
昭乃皇帝特别宠爱之人。第一位女作家。完成其兄之工作（作前汉书）作文戒七篇

班雄
纪元后103年左右，继其父志，统辖西域。

班勇
—131
纪元后107年左右远征帕米尔地带。

班始
—130
领兵征伐西藏人。

第九章　汉朝的文化

汉朝的两个大历史家

　　以前说过秦始皇烧书杀儒家的故事。为什么他要这么作哪？他的目的是要杀所有反对他的人，可是书是烧不完的，儒家也是杀不完的。到了汉朝有许多学者，把他们以前背过的古书，又写出来了。又从房墙里找出来许多古书，所以汉朝的文化还是很有名。现在要讲两个汉朝的历史家，一个是司马迁一个是班固。司马迁是汉武帝时候的人。他写了一部历史，叫作史记。这部史记是中国第一部最有系统的历史书，不但在历史上的贡献很大，因为司马迁的文章写的好，就是在文学上的贡献也很不小。司马迁死了以后，过了一百多年，又有一位班固写了一部前汉书，文章写的也很好。可是这部前汉书不是班固一个人写的。起头一部分是他的父亲班彪写的，他的父亲死了，皇帝叫班固接着往下写汉朝的历史。他写了多年，还没写完就死了。最后一部分是他的妹妹班昭写的。所有有学问的中国人跟研究中国学问的外国人，都知道史记跟汉书这两部书。

汉朝的宗教

　　以上我们讲过周朝有儒，道，墨，法四个学派。墨家在周朝的后期消灭了。法家在秦朝势力很大，以后他的势力慢慢的

26

小了。汉朝的皇帝有的喜欢儒家。用儒家的思想办理国政。有的喜欢道家，用道家的思想办理国政。儒家跟道家只是两个学派，到了汉朝道家变成了一种宗教。儒家经过汉武帝和汉光武的提倡以后，势力才大起来。慢慢的这个学派变成国教。儒家跟道家都是中国本国的。汉朝又从外国得到一种宗教，就是印度的佛教。张骞通西域的时候，就知道南边有一个国家叫做印度，也听说印度有一种宗教叫做佛教。

中国历史上有一个故事，关于佛教来到中国的事情。汉光武的儿子汉明帝，有一天作梦，梦见一个金人身上发光，在宫殿里飞来飞去。他醒了就问他的大臣。大臣们告诉他，这是印度的佛。他就派人到印度去把佛书带回来了，翻成中文。这是佛教第一次到中国。以后相信佛教的人，就慢慢的多起来了。这个故事，虽然不是很可靠的证据，也可以表明佛教是在后汉朝来到中国的。

中 国 有 名 之 司 马 氏

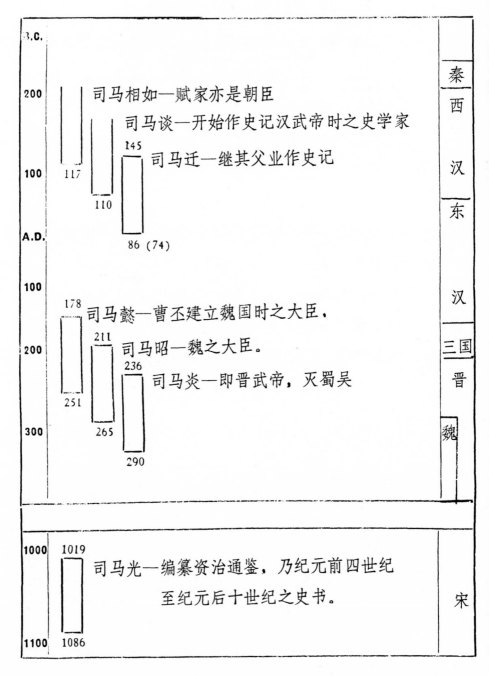

司马相如—赋家亦是朝臣

司马谈—开始作史记汉武帝时之史学家

司马迁—继其父业作史记

司马懿—曹丕建立魏国时之大臣，

司马昭—魏之大臣。

司马炎—即晋武帝，灭蜀吴

司马光—编纂资治通鉴，乃纪元前四世纪
至纪元后十世纪之史书。

秦 西汉 东汉 三国 晋 魏 宋

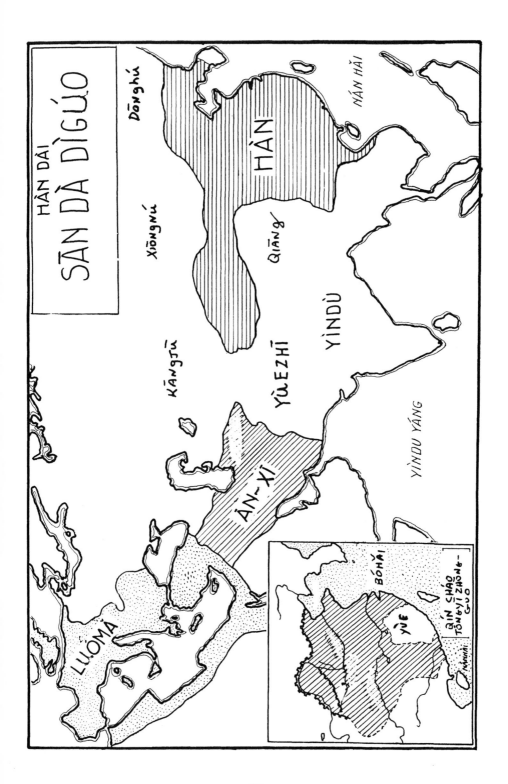

HÀN ĐẠI
SÃN DÃ DÌGUÓ

Dōnghú

NÁN HÃI

HÀN

Xiōngnú

Qiāng

YÌNDÙ

Kāngjū

YÙEZHĪ

YÌNDÙ YÁNG

AN–XI

LUÓMA

BÓHÃI

YÚE

QÍN CHÁO
TÓNGYĪ ZHŌNG-
GUO

NHHH

29

第十章　三　国

汉朝的末年

汉朝灭亡以前三十几年，国内很乱。　在一八四年，发生黄巾的造反。这个黄巾派的人，是反对朝代。就利用宗教的名义，达到他们的目的，所以历史上说是道教反对儒教。另外还有平民造反。因为田地都在地主的手里，老百姓摸不着生活。这次造反没成功，可是大臣们趁着这个机会，把军队势力都得到他们手里，从此以后汉朝就可以说没有势力了。那时候最有势力的一位大臣叫董卓。当时皇帝是个小孩子，不能够自己管理国家的事情。董卓用他的名义来管理政治。因为他怕别的大臣们，董卓把洛邑城给烧了，又往回迁都到长安。在一九二年被他手下的一个大将杀了。董卓死了以后，有一位大将名叫曹操发展势力，想作皇帝。他抓住汉朝的皇帝，也象董卓用皇帝的名义，打别的想作皇帝的人。要是把别人都打倒了，皇帝自然就是他的了。

中国分成三个国家

曹操用的这个法子很成功，十几年里头他打倒了很多地盘大军队多的人。只有两位没有被他打倒。一位是孙权，一位是刘备。二百〇八年曹操带了八十万军队去打他们。孙权跟刘备

联合起来在湖北赤壁跟曹操打了一个大仗。这仗就是历史上有名的赤壁战争。这仗以后曹操就没有力量统一中国了。中国从这个时候起就分作三个国家了。

关　羽

　　刘备的势力在赤壁战争以前很小，在赤壁战争以后就慢慢的大起来。二一九年他派一个大将—关羽—从湖南去打曹操。关羽打的很好，曹操害怕得了不得。那时候孙权想要刘备的湖南跟湖北的地盘。　他就跟曹操联合起来打关羽。没有多少时候，湖南跟湖北被孙权抢去了。关羽也被孙权杀了。

分三个国家

　　关羽死后的第二年。—二百二十年—曹操也死了。曹操的儿子曹丕就把汉朝的皇帝推翻，自己作了魏国的皇帝。刘备跟孙权听到这个消息也跟着作了蜀国跟吴国的皇帝。这就是三国时代的魏国，蜀国，吴国，三个国家。

二二〇至二六五

　　蜀国的刘备作了皇帝以后，很恨吴国的皇帝孙权。二百二十年，他带了许多兵打吴国，可是被吴国打的大败。第二年刘备就死了。他的儿子刘禅，小名儿叫阿斗，作了蜀国的皇帝。

那时候刘禅才十七岁，是个没有用的人。可是蜀国有一个好大
臣，叫诸葛亮。他不但帮助刘备作了皇帝又保护刘备的儿子作
了十来年皇帝。刘备死了以后，诸葛亮知道蜀国的敌国不是吴
国，是势力大推翻汉朝的魏国。他就跟吴国讲和，常常出兵打
魏国。半年里出兵七次，每次都得胜了。可是蜀国的地方太小，
军队不多，不能把魏国打倒。二三四年诸葛亮最后一次出兵打
魏国的时候，就在军队里生病死了。蜀国的人民听见这消息，
没有一个不伤心的。

司马炎成立晋国

诸葛亮死了以后，蜀国跟吴国的势力一天比一天小，魏国
的势力一天比一天大。可是这时候魏国的势力不在曹家的皇帝
手里，在魏国的一个大臣手里。这家的大臣姓司马。二百六十
三年司马昭把蜀国灭了。二百六十五年，他的儿子司马炎把魏
国推翻，自己作了皇帝。这就是晋朝的头一个皇帝—晋武帝。
等到二百八十年，晋武帝—就是司马炎—把吴国灭了以后，中
国全国又统一了。

第十一章　三国的名人

曹操梦里杀人

大家都知道曹操是一个会用兵的人。中国有一句俗话「说到曹操，曹操就到」这句俗话就是说曹操用兵快的意思。可是在中国历史上，曹操是一个坏人，因为他的心狠毒，坏主意很多。他老怕他的敌人在他睡觉的时候害死他。他就对人说：「我睡觉的时候，你们不要到我面前来，因为我在梦里会杀人，」有一次他睡在床上，被窝掉下去了。他的佣人过去替他拿被窝，他就坐起来了。一刀把他的佣人杀死，躺下又睡了。过了一会儿他醒了，就对别的佣人说「我不知道是我梦里杀死的」后来人都以为曹操在梦里真会杀人，在他睡觉的时候，就不敢到他床前去了。

曹操借人头

又有一次他跟人打仗，他的军粮不多了，他叫他的管军粮的官少发一点儿军粮。后来军粮官对他说：「兵吃的太少不满意，怎么办呢？曹操想了一想就说：「我跟你借一件东西，」军粮官说「借什么？」曹操说：「你的头。」军粮官说：「我没有作错事。」曹操不等他说完了话，就把他杀了。拿了他的头对兵说：「军粮官偷了军粮，所以你们吃的不多。我现在已经把他杀了」。兵真以为军粮官偷了军粮，很恨军粮官，就没人不满意曹操了。

桃园三结义

刘备是蜀国的第一个皇帝，因为他姓刘，他说他跟汉朝皇帝是一家人。在他小的时候，他父亲死了，家里很穷，他跟母亲卖草鞋。他长大了碰见两个人，一个是推小车子关羽，一个是卖肉的张飞。三个人就在张飞家的后院子里，做了不同姓的弟兄。刘备老大。关羽老二，张飞老三。这就是有名的桃园三结义。三个人做了兄弟以后就去当兵。白日一块儿吃饭，晚上一块儿睡觉。后来刘备作了皇帝，关羽和张飞都帮了他不少忙。

刘备在中国历史上是个好人，因为他扶助汉朝的皇帝，他对人民很好，可是他也是个很有主意的人。有一次他在曹操那儿。汉朝的皇帝叫他打倒曹操，可是没有机会。他又怕曹操知道，他就在家里种菜，为的是叫曹操不注意他。有一天曹操请他喝酒，就问他，「你到的地方很多，你知道谁是有本领的人，」刘备说了这个人，曹操说不是。又说了那个人，曹操也说不是。后来曹操说：「现在有本领的人，只有两个，一个是你一个是我」。刘备吓坏了，以为曹操知道了他的秘密。他手里拿的筷子也掉在地下了。又怕曹操疑惑。正好这个时候打了一个大雷，刘备说：「这个雷真大，把我的筷子也吓掉了」。说完了这个话，两个人一笑。曹操也就没有疑惑他。

关羽先打敌人后喝酒

孔子是中国的一位文圣人。中国还有一位武圣人，就是以前推小车子的关羽。古时候中国打仗都是将对将打，兵对兵打。大将骑着马，用一个很长的兵器，打别的大将。关羽长的很有个样子。他用的一把刀，有八十多斤重。他骑的一匹马，一天可以走一千里。

有一次刘备，曹操，还有别的人，联合起来打另外一位董卓。董卓有一位大将很厉害，没有人打的过他。关羽要打他去，他们这边的长官不许他去，因为那个时候关羽地位太小。只是一个排长的样子。曹操在旁边说：「这个人的样子长的不错，也许有本领。为什么不叫他试一试呢？曹操就倒了一杯热酒给他喝，关羽说：「等我杀了敌人的大将，再来喝酒」。他一出去就把敌人的大将杀了。等到他回来的时候，酒还没凉哪。

不忘旧交

关羽是中国的武圣人。这不是因为他的本领大，是因为他作好人。纪元后二百年曹操把刘备打的大败。关羽跟刘备家里的人，被曹操围在一个土山上。曹操叫关羽投降，关羽说：「我现在不知道刘备在那儿住，要是我将来知道他住在什么地方，你得让我回到他那儿去。这样我才投降」。曹操很喜欢关羽，就答应了。关羽投降以后，曹操对他很好。叫他作大将。隔着

三天五天的，就请他吃一回饭。又给他很多的金银东西，跟那匹千里马。关羽也给曹操打了一次胜仗。　后来他知道了刘备住的地方，他就把曹操给他的一切都留下了。他不告诉曹操，就带着刘备的家眷，找刘备去了。曹操手下的人，劝曹操派兵追他。曹操说：算了吧！让他去吧，这个人不忘旧交，就是把他追回来也没有用。

诸葛亮借箭

　　曹操是三国时代一个会用兵的人，可是诸葛亮比曹操更会用兵。在赤壁战争的时候，曹操在长江北岸，刘备跟孙权在长江南岸。两边在江里打仗，用的箭很多，可是刘备跟孙权没有多少箭。有一天晚上天很黑，又下了大雾。诸葛亮想了一个主意。他用二十只大船，每一个船上装满了草作的人。夜里从南岸开到北岸。快到北岸的时候，他就叫兵打起鼓来。曹操听见鼓声，吓坏了。不知道来了多少兵。又在雾里什么都看不见，只好叫他的兵对着鼓声放箭。诸葛亮打了一夜的鼓，曹操放了一夜的箭。天快亮了，雾快没有了，船上的箭也快装满了。诸葛亮叫他的兵高声叫：「谢谢曹操的箭」。就把船开回南岸。曹操知道受了欺骗，派船去追，已经追不上了。诸葛亮到了南岸，把草人身上的箭拔下来数了一数，一共有十万多箭。这么一来，刘备跟孙权就得了很多的箭。

空城计

　　曹操死了以后。诸葛亮常常带着蜀国的兵，去打魏国。有一次他的军队在前线，他自己在一个小城里，手下只有一百多个没用的兵。这时候魏国有一个大将，带了两万兵到了城下。诸葛亮心里想，「打是打不过他们，要逃走也来不及了」。他叫四个老兵，在城门口扫地。他自己带两个小兵，在城楼上喝酒弹琴，琴声里他对魏国兵说：「你们到了这里，为什么不进城呢」？魏国的大将看见这样子很奇怪，他心里想，「诸葛亮是个会用兵的人。他把城门大开，城里头一定有很多的兵。我不要上他的当」。他就带着军队回去了。走到半路才知道城里没有兵。知道诸葛亮用的是一个空城计。他就气的了不得。这时候前线的蜀国兵已经回来了。把他打的大败。

THE THREE KINGDOMS

三 国 历 史

第十二章　晋朝跟南北朝

晋　朝

司马炎统一了中国以后，平定了三十多年。可是晋朝的皇帝没有汉朝的皇帝强。并且北边的鞑子越来越厉害。因为黄河一带常常受鞑子的侵略，晋朝的皇帝在三百一十七年把京城搬到南边去了。这是头一次南京作了中国的京城。从这时候起，晋朝就没有势力保守黄河一带地。有一种鞑子名叫拓跋，在中国北边立了魏国「这不是三国时代的魏国，这也叫北魏」。

移民的结果

中国北方有许多人不喜欢受鞑子的管理，就搬到南边长江一带住去了。当然这些搬家的人，不是老百姓。穷人不容易逃走。搬家的人多半是贵族，是有钱的人，是有学问的人。那时候长江流域的文化，比不上黄河流域的文化。所以这个人民搬家的事情，表明长江流域的文化很进步。

可是从这一件事也发生了一个难题。人数一多了，粮食就不够吃了。得想法子多出产。好在北方来的人民懂得灌溉，就教南方的人造运河挖水沟。运河有两样的用处：一面是运粮食，一面是浇田地。从那时候起，长江口岸那一带地很发达。

佛 教

　　第三世纪到第六世纪是佛教在中国发展的时候。不但有印度人来到中国传佛教，也有中国人做佛教的和尚，到印度去，为的是研究佛教。这些留学生，带回许多佛教的书，到中国来翻成了中国文。有的人也记下了他们在路上所遇见的事情。他们的记录是很重要的。因为印度的历史学家很少。印度人不注重作史书。要是没有这些中国旅行家所写的记录，这个时代的印度历史就不可靠了。

法 显

　　最有名的旅行家名叫法显，是佛教的一个和尚。他在三百九十九年起身，走了西域的南路。因为很穷没有多少钱作路费，他就走的很慢。他得到信佛的城去求帮助。这一路上佛教的人送他钱给他饭吃，给他地方住三两天。这样他慢慢的经过南路，走了一万多里才到了印度。

　　在路上法显天天记下他所看见的，所经过的事情，作了一本记录。到了一个城，他就记下这个城的名字，人数，人家，言语，政治，出产。这些事情他都写在记录上带回中国来了。法显在印度住了十四年。回家的时候，不是又打西域那么回来的；是坐船回到中国一个海口，从那儿走路回到长安。

第十三章　佛教的影响

中国文化受了佛教很大的影响。以前中国的雕刻是很简单的，也不很多。佛教很注重用石头雕刻佛象。这个石象放在佛教的庙里。有的象是非常美的，有的象是顶大的。离山西省的大同不远有大山洞，北魏朝的时候这些山洞做为庙用。洞里的佛象是从山面刻出来的。有四五丈高。这就是有名的「云冈石佛」。这些佛象都是在第五世纪（四百五十五至四百九十九）造的。

这时代中国画家也画了很美的佛象。并且有几位诗家。第一位就是陶潜，（三百六十五至四百二十七）他的诗有不少已经翻成英文了。

由佛教带来的损失

从别的方面来看，中国的经济受了佛教很大的损失。有很多的中国人，因为当时的内乱，离开职业了，做了佛教的和尚。这些人离开社会，住在庙里。他们对社会就没多大功用了。社会里做买卖的、种庄家的，跟工人太少了。有两三次皇帝因为这个缘故叫全国的庙都关门，下命令叫和尚们都回到社会去做事。

文化东传

这个时代不但有佛教传到中国，也有中国的文化传到高丽

41

和日本两国。高丽国是在中国东北边。战国时代，有一个燕国侵略东北一直到鸭绿江，就是现在中国和高丽的分界。从那时候中国文化就传到高丽，从高丽又慢慢的传到日本。那时候的日本不象现在，人数又很少，国家又不统一。有许多小国常常彼此打仗。日本受了中国文化的影响以后才成了一国。

地　图

有这么些个旅行家，当然地理学要进步。在第四世纪有一位名叫裴秀（二百二十四至二百七十一）给晋武帝画了一个中国全国图。这个图上画的有山，河，湖，海。有省界也有大城。以前没有这么详细的地图。

茶

你们知道中国人都喝茶。喝茶的这个风俗是从中国起的。我们不知谁发明茶是可喝的，也不知道是什么时候发明的。有一篇中国文章，是二百七十三年写的，提到喝茶。原来人看茶是一种药水，不可以随便喝。到了纪元后第四世纪，在长江一带有许多贵族人喝茶。慢慢的这个风俗也传到别的地方去了。中国北部的人直到第十二世纪才喝茶，印度人是从中国学的这个风俗。到了第十七世纪，西国人也就从中国得了茶叶。

「茶」这个字在中国最古的字典—尔雅—上已经有了。在汉朝的各种书里也常常看见这个字。在吴国没亡以前，有一个

皇帝常请大臣们喝酒。有一位不能喝酒，用「茶」代替。后来
到了唐朝有一个人叫陆羽，他很喜欢喝茶。他作了一本书—茶
经—提到茶的起源，做茶的法子，跟喝茶所用的家俱：都很详
细。从那时候起，喝茶就成了风俗了。他死了以后，都称他为
「茶神」。

是不是黑暗时代

有的外国人说，这是中国的黑暗时代，很象欧洲第八世纪
的黑暗时代。国内实在是不平。很多小国常常打仗。中国的势
力也不象汉朝那么大。可是一看以上所说的些个大贡献，就不
能管这个时代叫黑暗时代，因为文化的进步实在是不小。

CHINA AROUND 500 A.D.
∴ Buddhist cave temples

第十四章　隋朝　五八九—六一八

隋朝跟秦朝的比较

你们也许还记得秦始皇建立了秦朝。那个朝代的历史，虽然是很短的—不过有十四年—可是工作很多。在历史上的地位很重要。在第六世纪末期，中国又乱了。有很多小国打来打去，谁也不肯让谁。后来又统一起来了，就叫隋朝。隋朝的历史也不很长，是从五百八十九年到六百十八年。可是隋朝的工作也是很要紧的。

造运河

秦始皇造了万里长城。头一个隋朝的皇帝就是杨坚—把以前所造的小运河给连起来了，做成现在的大运河。造成了就可以把长江一带的食粮运到北方去。湖南省出的米最多。这个米可以用船运到南京。从南京走运河一直到黄河。这样的交通当然对于中国统一跟商业的问题很有关系。

图书馆

杨坚的儿子杨广也很有本事。他也是象秦始皇，多加了一道长城在秦朝的长城南边。他可是跟秦始皇有一个大分别。秦始皇烧了书，杀了文士，杨广开了一个大图书馆。存起来多少万书。他叫文士们抄写古书，又派了很多人抄写新近的书。那

44

时候印刷的方法刚在发明，用木版刻书，不过还不能通行，所以每一本书是人慢慢的抄写的。

外 交

杨坚的外交也有很多的结果。在南方他打到越南。西北边他又开了南北路，使中国的买卖人又可以通商到中亚洲。这些计划都成功了，所以杨坚觉得他是打不败的。以后就注意到东北方。东北有一个高丽国占辽宁省的南部跟朝鲜的北部。地盘不小，也有相当的国力。杨坚派兵攻打这个国，就碰了一个钉子。后来杨广自己派了兵去打他，也打的大败，就把兵撤进长城来了。

隋朝灭亡

隋朝两个皇帝的这些大工作不能不叫老百姓受苦。挖运河的时候，用的工人一共有三百六十万。当然人民不满意。皇帝在别的工作上花的钱也很多。杨坚（文帝）跟他的儿子杨广（炀帝）造了三个京城。两个是以前作过京城的长安和洛阳。第三个是靠近黄河口的扬州。人民受不了这样的苦，就革命了。有一家姓李的—父亲叫李渊，儿子叫李世民。他们父子推翻了隋朝，在六百十八年立了唐朝。

在战国时代行政是很简单的，因为国家小地盘不大，人数也少。秦始皇一统一了全国，行政就很复杂，成了大难题。汉朝的行政是很宽的。从汉朝到隋朝有二百五十来年的内乱。这么一来大家都注意中央行政的方法。要是政府没有势力就没人管社会的三个重要问题：

一、国家统一问题。

二、全国交通的问题。

三、食粮分配的问题。

在这些事情上隋朝的两个皇帝做了很多的工作，所以他们在这方面有很大的贡献。

第十五章　唐朝　六一八—九〇七

唐朝跟汉朝的比较

以前我们说过，隋朝象秦朝。一看唐朝的历史，就觉得隋朝以后的唐朝跟以后的汉朝有三个相同的地方：

一、汉朝跟唐朝的历史都很长。汉朝有四百多年的历史。唐朝从纪元后六百十八年到九百〇七年也差不多有三百年的样子。

二、汉唐都是中国很强盛的时代，所以我们有时候管中国人叫汉人或唐人。

三、汉朝灭亡以后，中国分做三个国家。到了晋朝才又统一起来。唐朝灭亡以后，中国分做十个国家。到了宋朝才又统一起来。

唐太宗

唐朝的第一个皇帝是唐高祖—李渊—可是唐朝这一朝不是李渊打下来的。隋朝的末年，隋炀帝住在扬州。中国国内乱的很。有势力的人都独立了。那时候李渊是山西的一个官。李世民也劝他的父亲独立。起头李渊不肯，后来想了一想，觉得李世民的话也不错。就对李世民说：「你要独立，我们就独立吧！以后灭家亡身是你，变家成国也是你。现在完全瞧你的了」

李渊独立以后就派李世民去打隋炀帝的两个京城，洛阳跟长安。六百十八年李世民把洛阳跟长安打下来了。隋炀帝在扬州也被人杀了。李渊就在长安作了唐朝的皇帝。可是那时候，中国还是乱的很。还有许多大大小小的国家。李世民就带着兵，今天打这国，明天打那国。到了六百二十六年李渊老了，让李世民做了皇帝，中国才成了一统。

武则天 Wu Zetian

唐太宗—李世民—是中国历史上一个有名的皇帝，因为他不但会打仗，统一中国，并且也很爱百姓，把国里的事情管理的很好。唐太宗死了以后，他的儿子唐高宗 Gaozong 做了皇帝。高宗这个人也不错。在六百六十五那一年，他把高丽灭了。可是他有一个毛病，他太相信他的皇后武则天。在唐高宗做皇帝的时期，武则天的势力已经很大了。六百八十三年唐高宗死了，皇后的势力就更大了。她不让她的儿子继位 jiwei~succeed to the throne，自己做了皇帝。

武则天是一个很能干的女人，也是中国历史上第一个女人做皇帝。可是她的心很毒，因为她自己的儿子反对她，她就把她儿子杀了。后来她又杀了很多皇帝家里 imperial family 的人。她很有学问。她自己造了十九个中国字，可是后来没有人用。七百〇四年她已经八十一岁了。她的大臣们把她推翻，请她的儿子唐中宗 Zhongzong 做皇帝。

唐明皇

唐中宗是个没有用的人。他做了六年多的皇帝，就被他的皇后——韦后——害死了。韦后跟武则天一样，也想自己做皇帝。可是这次皇帝家有一个人带兵。把韦后杀了。这个人是唐朝另外一个有名的皇帝——明皇。

明皇是个有能力的皇帝。起头他做了许多对人民有好处的事情。后来他得到一个妃子叫杨贵妃。他很爱这个妃子，就不管国里的事情。那时候有一个鞑子叫安禄山，是一个大军官。管着山西，河北一带的地方。他见过杨贵妃好几次，很喜欢贵妃，贵妃也喜欢他。七百五十四年他就带兵打进长安，想把这个贵妃抢过来，可是这个时候杨贵妃不在长安，已经被唐明皇带着上四川了。

在明皇带走杨贵妃往四川去的时候，军士们都很恨杨贵妃。有一天军士忽然停住不走了。明皇问是什么缘故。军士们说：「这次安禄山打进长安都是为的贵妃；不杀贵妃，军士们不愿意到四川去。明皇想来想去，没有法子，就派人把贵妃勒死了。贵妃死了以后，明皇伤心的了不得。一直到死，他还是很想这个贵妃。

唐朝的灭亡

唐明皇到了四川以后，他的儿子——唐肃宗——把安禄山打平

了，可是从这时候起，唐朝地方官的势力就慢慢的大起来了。
到了九百〇七年有一个地方官—朱温—把唐朝灭了，成立了梁
朝。以后在五十三年之内，中国的北方前后换了五个朝代：后
梁，后唐，后晋，后汉，后周。中国的南方又分做十个国家。
到了九百六十年，宋太祖—赵匡胤—才又把中国统一起来。

Zhu Wen (handwritten above 朱温)
Liang Chao (handwritten left of 朝)
Zhao Kuang Yin (handwritten below 赵匡胤)

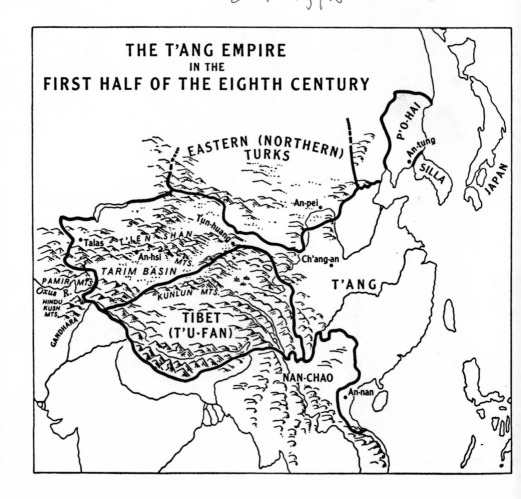

THE T'ANG EMPIRE
IN THE
FIRST HALF OF THE EIGHTH CENTURY

P'O-HAI
An-tung
SILLA
JAPAN
EASTERN (NORTHERN) TURKS
An-pei
Tun-huang
Talas
T'IEN SHAN MTS.
An-hsi
Ch'ang-an
TARIM BASIN
PAMIR MTS.
Oxus R.
HINDU KUSH MTS.
GANDHARA
KUNLUN MTS.
T'ANG
TIBET
(T'U-FAN)
NAN-CHAO
An-nan

第十六章　唐朝的外交

唐朝的国界

以前我们讲过汉朝的国界是很大的。唐朝的国界比汉朝的国界更大。在唐朝最强盛的时候，唐朝的东边到海跟朝鲜、西边到帕米尔山，南边到安南，北边到贝加尔湖。在讲唐朝国界的时候，还有三件事可以讲一讲。

一、唐朝打朝鲜。

二、唐朝跟日本的关系。

三、唐朝跟西方的交通。

唐朝打朝鲜

你们知道隋炀帝打高丽，被高丽打败了。后来唐太宗打高丽，也没有把高丽打下来。高丽只是朝鲜的一个国家。除了高丽以外，朝鲜还有两个国家；一个是百济，一个是新罗。百济是日本的属国，新罗是中国的属国。唐太宗以后，唐高宗作了皇帝。他派他的一个大将去打百济，在百济的白江口这个地方，中国的军队跟日本的军队遇着了。中国的军队把日本的军队打的大败。打沉了四百多只日本船，又杀了许多的日本人，海水都变红了。在六百六十三年那一年把百济灭了。六百六十八那一年又把高丽灭了。朝鲜全部又作了中国的土地。

唐朝跟日本

　　从汉朝到唐朝中国管日本叫做「倭国」。日本称自己的国叫「大和」，所以日本文也叫和文，日本衣服也叫和服。第四世纪末年，日本从中国学会了造酒跟织布的法子，又把孔子的书带到日本去，日本人才知道读书识字。以后日本国王给隋炀帝写信，他称自己是「日出处天子」，称隋炀帝是「日没处天子」。这两句话的意思就是「出太阳地方的皇帝」跟「落太阳地方的皇帝」。隋炀帝看了很不高兴。他给日本国王写回信，第一句写的是「皇帝问倭王」。后来日本被唐朝打败了，日本常常派人到中国来进贡，又派学生来念书。这个时候他们知道「倭」字的意思是「小人」的意思，不好听，就把「日出处天子」的「日出处」三个字改作「日本」两个字。用日本这两个字作了他们国家的名字。

唐朝跟西方的交通

　　在唐朝时代，东方有一个大国那就是中国。西方也有一个大国，那就是回回国。那个时候有些个唐朝的中国人到东罗马帝国的君士坦丁城去做买卖。回回国的阿拉伯人，也常常到中国的广州，杭州跟扬州来做买卖。阿拉伯人到中国来的路有两条：一条是从西北边陆路上来；一条是从南边海上来。这个中

国人跟阿拉伯人做买卖，对于两边都有好处。西方学了中国养蚕的法子，跟造纸的法子。西方的人又买了很多中国的磁器。中国从西方新得到十来种吃的东西，从印度跟阿拉伯学了算学跟医学。中国的磁器匠也学了些个希腊．波斯，印度的画画儿的式样。

第十七章　唐朝的文化

文　学

唐朝的国界不但很大，唐朝的文化也很发达。唐朝的文化可以分做文学美术宗教三部分。

唐朝时代是中国诗最好的时代，以后没有一个时代的诗可以比得上唐朝的。唐朝有许多有名的诗人。最有名的两个人是李白跟杜甫。所有研究中国学问的人都知道这两位中国大诗人。

唐朝的「文」就是我们常说的「文理」或是「文言」，也是很重要的。后来的中国文人从唐朝跟宋朝的文学家里挑出来八个人。把这八个人写的文章做样子。这就叫「唐宋八家」。这八个人，第一就是唐朝的韩愈。在那个时候有一个「古文运动」就是他提倡的。这种势力后来很大。后来念书的人都受了他的影响。经过宋，元，明，清，到民国已经有一千多年了。直到胡适博士的白话文运动起来，古文的势力才打破了。现在我们常说的「白话文」就是对「古文」说的。

美　术

　　唐朝的人除了做诗以外，又很会写字跟画画儿，唐朝的画家—就是会写美字的人—很多。现在中国人学写字，在初学的时候，多数还是学唐朝几个书家写字的法子。唐朝的画家也不少，以前中国画家只画人物，画山水的很少。中国的山水画儿到了唐朝就很好了，可是一切的方法直到了宋朝才算完全。

　　在唐朝的画家里面，有一个人叫吴道子，画佛象最有名。有人说：「吴道子画的佛象，鬼见了，都是怕的」。

　　雕刻或是塑象在唐朝也很进步。在唐明皇的时候，有一个人叫杨惠之，他跟吴道子是同学。当初他们两个人一块儿学画画儿，可是他赶不上吴道子，所以他就改学塑象了。在这个事情上他是第一个出了名的人。当时各大庙的佛象都是他做的。他也会在墙上作山水。现在他所作的佛象，在苏州的一个庙里还有几个。

　　唐明皇不但是一位有名的皇帝，并且也是一位音乐家。因为他很懂音乐所以那时候的音乐特别的发达。他很爱戏剧。他成立了一个戏剧学校，叫「梨园」学生有好几百，男女都有。到现在中国唱戏的，都拿唐明皇当戏神。

唐朝的宗教

　　唐朝时代中国已经有了儒，道，佛三个宗教。这三个宗教

在唐朝很发达。唐朝的皇帝说是道教李耳的后人，所以他们常
常帮道教的忙。有好几个皇帝也很相信道教。唐太宗时代有一
个和尚叫唐玄奘，到印度去研究佛学。又带回许多书到中国来，
译成中文。从那个时候以后，相信佛教的更多了。那个女皇帝
武则天，也是相信佛教的一个人。

　　除了以上的三种宗教，唐朝又从西方得到三种宗教。那就
是波斯国的火教，景教跟回教。火教是波斯人的国教。景教是
耶稣教的一种。回教是阿拉伯人在第七世纪发生的一种新宗教。
只有回教对于中国的关系很大。现在在中国至少有两千万回教
人。可是这三种宗教没有儒，道，佛，三种宗教发达。

第十八章　宋朝

北宋跟南宋

在前几课我们所念的汉朝分西汉跟东汉，晋朝分西晋东晋。可是到了宋朝，不分东西，分南北了。宋朝的历史是从九百六十年，到一千二百七十九年。一共有三百多年的历史。在这三百多年当中，我们可以把他分作两个时期。第一个时期是从九百六十年，到一千一百二十七年。第二个时期，是从一千一百二十七年到一千二百七十九年。因为第一个时期，宋朝的京城是在北方的河南开封。第二期是在南方的浙江杭州，所以中国历史上称第一期叫北宋，称第二期叫南宋。

北　宋

宋朝的第一个皇帝，是宋太祖（赵匡胤），他本来是后周朝的一个大将。后来后周的老皇帝死了，赵匡胤就把后周的小皇帝推翻，在开封自己作了皇帝。他是中国历史上一个有能力的皇帝。他很爱老百姓，对于大臣们也很好。在他做皇帝时候，中国分作十来个国家。他今天打这个国，明天打那个国，灭了许多国家。宋太祖知道唐朝的灭亡是因为地方官的势力太大，所以他用种种的法子，慢慢的把地方官的势力拿到中央政府的手里来。他又叫各地方把老弱的兵留下，把强壮的兵都送到中

56

央政府。这么一来，地方就永不能反抗中央了。在另一方面，他又派专管财政的人到各地方去，把应用的钱留下，把敷余的都送到中央去。九百七十六年他死了。他把皇帝给了他的弟弟宋太宗，（赵匡义）。那时候，中国还有两个国家，没有被宋朝打下来。等到赵匡义作了皇帝，把这两个国家灭了以后，中国才完全统一。

宋辽的关系

他又想，趁着这个机会把在北方的辽国赶出中国去，就亲自带着兵去打他们，可是没想到被辽国打的大败。从此以后宋朝跟外国的冲突，就一天比一天厉害起来了。这个辽国从前叫契丹，到了九百三十七年才改了叫「辽」，同时也就在北平这个地方开始建立了京城，名字就叫「燕京」。

大政治家王安石

到了第六个皇帝，宋神宗，才想要改良政治。就用了一个很有学问的人，王安石，做他的宰相。王安石教了宋神宗许多强国的法子，例如：

一、改良税收的法子。国家每一年要用的钱要先作预算。

二、叫人民多种没有人种的地。要是人民没有本钱，政府借给他们，等他们有钱的时候再还给政府。

三、米价贱的时候，政府把米买进来。等到米贵的时候，政府再用贱价卖给人民。

四、唐朝以前中国是用征兵制，所有的老百姓都当兵。宋朝的时候中国用的是募兵制。兵是人民的一种职业。王安石把宋朝的募兵制改作征兵制。

五、宋朝的兵器都是地方上造，造好了送给中央政府。所以有的好有的坏，有的大有的小，王安石不叫地方上造兵器，叫地方上把钱送给政府，政府找好工人自己造。

王安石还有许多强国的法子，一直到现在中国还有用哪。可是在宋朝的时代，那些只喜欢说话不喜欢做事的大臣们看见王安石今天出一个新法子，明天又出一个新法子，都不喜欢他。想出种种的话来反对他。王安石虽然作了九年的宰相，宋神宗也很相任他。可是因为反对他的人太多，他的那些好法子用起来都没有什么结果。

这时候最大的困难是财政，因为宋朝从开国以来就不断的跟外国打仗。每年把国家进的钱三分之二都用在军事上了，并且每年还要送给外国很多的钱跟东西。北宋的皇帝跟大臣们又都是能说不能行，所以财政到了那种困难的地步，也没有人肯出来负责整理。

从那时候起所有北宋的大臣分成两党，一个是「新党」，

一个是「旧党」。新党的领袖自然是王安石。旧党的领袖就是那位作「资治通鉴」的历史学家司马光。

过了几年宋神宗死了，一切的新法也都停止了。没有人用王安石的法子了。新旧两党闹的越来越厉害，北宋也就一天比一天坏下去了。

北宋的灭亡

宋神宗以后，宋哲宗作了皇帝。宋哲宗以后，宋徽宗作了皇帝。宋徽宗是一个很聪明的人。他做的诗，写的字，画的画儿，都很好，可是他不喜欢管理国家的事，又很爱花钱。那个时候人民的生活苦的很；所以有人说：「宋徽宗什么都好，就是不是一个好皇帝。宋神宗什么都不好，就是是一个好皇帝」。

在宋徽宗的时候，中国的东北方有一个国家叫金国强起来，常常来打中国。在一千一百二十五年把辽国灭了。宋朝的大臣们还是只说话不做事，不想法子来抵抗。一千一百二十六年宋徽宗把皇帝给了他的儿子，宋钦宗。第二年金国的兵又打进来了。在宋朝的大臣们讨论应当不应当迁都到南方去。金国的兵已经把开封打下来了，把宋朝的两个皇帝—宋徽宗跟宋钦宗—都抢去了。北宋也就在一千一百二十七年灭亡了。

第十九章　南　宋

在南方复兴

北宋灭亡以后，宋徽宗的第六个儿子，宋高宗，跑到南方，在浙江的杭州作了皇帝。这就是中国历史上的南宋。在南宋时期，中国的北方在金国的手里。南方在宋朝手里。金国还是常常来打宋朝，可是也没有把宋朝打下来。过了十来年宋朝的兵慢慢的强起来了。宋朝有一个大将常常把金国的兵打的大败。这个时候宋朝有些大臣不主张跟金国打仗，主张跟金国说和。以后的一百来年，金国没有力量把南宋打下来。南宋也没有力量把金国的兵打出中国的北方。

岳　飞

在南宋的大将里面有一个大将名叫岳飞，是一个很爱国的人，也是一个很好的大将。他跟金国的兵打了很多的胜仗，可是他还是不满意。他不但要把金国的兵打出中国，他还要把金国灭了。这个时候南宋的宰相是秦桧，是中国的历史上一个很坏很坏的人。他不主张跟金国打仗，主张跟金国说和。可是岳飞要跟金国打仗。怎么办？他心里想只要把岳飞杀了就没有人要跟金国打仗了。一千一百四十四年岳飞的军队把金国的兵打的大败。快要打到北宋的京城，河南开封的时候，秦桧把岳飞叫到杭州。说岳飞要造反，就把岳飞跟岳飞的儿子女婿都杀了。岳飞死了以后，人民伤心的了不得。南宋就再没有力量把金国的兵打出中国来。

岳飞是中国历史上一个有名的大将，跟三国时候的关羽是一样的有名。杭州城外有一个岳飞庙。那里有秦桧跟秦桧的妻子的石象都跪在地下。许多逛庙的人走到石象旁边的时候，都要打他们几下，踢他们几下。从这个地方你们可以看出中国人很恨不爱国的人。

南宋的灭亡

南宋跟金国说和以后，中国北方的蒙古人很强盛。一千二百三十四年南宋跟蒙古人联合起来把金国灭了。蒙古人就代替金国做了中国的新帝国。那个时候南宋有些个大臣们想把中国的北方从蒙古人手里拿回来，被蒙古人打的大败。以后蒙古人就常常派兵来。南宋的皇帝又作了蒙古人的俘虏了。可是南宋还没有灭亡，因为宋朝的皇帝家的一个人又在福建的福州做了皇帝。一千二百七十九年蒙古人把全中国都打下来了。南宋的皇帝跳到海里死了。南宋也就亡了。我们总起来看，宋朝三百多年到有二百多年是受外国人的侵略。

南宋的文化

宋朝人虽然不会打仗，可是宋朝有许多的历史学家，哲学家，跟文学家。研究中国学问的人，都知道中国有两种学问：一种是汉学，一种是宋学。这个宋学就是宋朝哲学家的学问。以前我们说过，宋朝人只会说话，不会做事。因为他们会说话，

所以他们也很会写文章。王安石的文章也写的不错。宋朝的人
除了写文章以外，又会做诗，还会做词。宋朝的人做的词跟唐
朝人做的诗一样—是没有一个朝代比得上的。中国文学史上常
说「唐诗，宋词」。这就是说：「诗是唐朝的最好，词是宋朝
的最好」。

教　育

宋朝的教育很发达，公立跟私立的学校都有。在中央还有
大学，也叫「国子监」。在这些学校以外还有专门研究别的功
课的地方，如：算学，医学，法律等等的。因为注重教育的结
果，所以「印刷」也特别的发达。在当时刻版印书的地方很多。
宋仁宗的时候「活字版」一出来，印刷的工作就更方便了。后
来这种法子传到西洋，对于欧洲的文明影响很大。

工商业

宋朝的工商业也很进步。工业里头最出名的是「瓷器」。
河北，河南，浙江几个地方所产的很好，可是在江西景德镇所
产的最出名。那时候跟外国做买卖的地方一共有五个，就是：
广州，杭州，泉州，跟青岛。外国来跟中国通商的有：日本，
高丽，印度，阿拉伯跟南洋群岛等国。

第二十章　元　朝

蒙古的建国

我们已经说过匈奴，拓跋，土耳其跟契丹这四种鞑子。看他们的历史，象是每几百年有一族游牧人兴起来。把沙漠地的一切小小的支派都联合起来。在汉朝时代有匈奴，在晋朝的时代有拓跋所立的魏国。在唐朝那时候土耳其种族侵略从辽河到里海，也常常跟唐朝捣乱。在第十二世纪中国北部叫东北的契丹人从宋朝的手里给抢了去了。

所以蒙古人在第十三世纪立国不过是第五次游牧鞑子兴起来。在一千二百〇六年所有的鞑子都在一个地方开他们的大年会。这个会选出一个铁木真作可汗，就是大王的意思。这个人在历史上称为成吉思汗。他很会用兵，又很会用人管理国家的事情。

成吉思汗的大工作

成吉思汗的头一个大工作，是把大沙漠南北一带地方的小国跟民族都统一起来了。第二是消灭中国西北部的夏国，就是西藏的（唐古特）人所立的一个国家。第三个工作是侵略东北部的金国。一千二百十四年打进他们的京城。后来在一千二百三十五年他的儿子窝阔台拿住了金国的末一个皇帝。把他杀了。金国的京城那时候叫燕京，就是现在的北平。

蒙古三次侵略西方

成吉思汗正要往南攻宋朝的时候，中亚洲的些个民族造反，杀死了好几百蒙古商人。所以在一千二百四十年，成吉思汗带着军队打到西方去了。他攻进了欧洲，打败了俄国的联军。后来他的一个儿子，窝阔台，在一千二百三十七年，派大将拔都把俄国的莫斯科打下来了。并且他过了喀尔巴千山，打进匈牙利国一直到多瑙河。末次是在一千二百五十八年。还有一个大将，名叫忽烈兀，侵略波斯国打进他们的京城报达。这几十年的时间，蒙人没有工夫攻击中国。成吉思死在一千二百二十七年。以后的几个可汗我们不能详详细细的讲。你可以看以下的「家系表」。成吉思的地盘分给他的四个儿子。这四个大国都承认窝阔台是他们的可汗，所以还是象一个大帝国的样子。

家系表

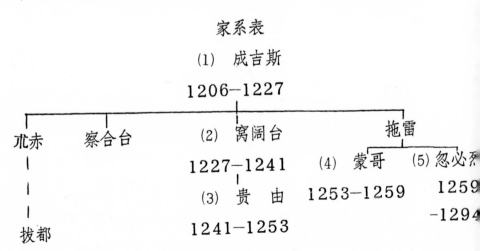

(1) 成吉斯
1206—1227

尤赤　　察合台　　(2) 窝阔台　　　　　拖雷
　　　　　　　　　1227—1241　　(4) 蒙哥　(5) 忽必烈
　　　　　　　　　(3) 贵由　　1253—1259　　1259
拔都　　　　　　　1241—1253　　　　　　　　—1294

忽必烈的工作

过了三十二年，成吉斯的一个孙子，名叫忽必烈，不按着选举的法子，就立自己作可汗。给他的国起了名字叫「元」国。那时候忽必烈是管理帝国东南部的汗。他做了可汗以后就想法子灭宋朝，可是这个目的也不是容易达到的。他先占了甘肃，四川，云南那带地，才敢攻击沿海的地方。到了一千二百七十六年他打进了宋朝的京城，就是杭州。又过了三年，宋朝的末一个皇帝在水里淹死了。

忽必烈这个人很能干，也很会用人。他知道蒙古人不大会办政治。他也知道中国人在这种事情上很有经验，可是他就怕他们造反。所以他派了些个中国人在帝国里的别的汗做官；又派了些个波斯人跟别处的人在中国做官。这样就不容易造反了。

忽必烈把中国全地得到了，还不认为满意。他还想侵略。听说东方有些个海岛叫做日本，他就想把这个地方也得到手里。因为蒙古人不会造船，也不会航海。他不得不叫中国人给他造船，给他当水手。中国人当然看不出来这个侵略日本的事情对于他们有什么益处，所以他们不能尽力的给蒙古皇帝打仗。

蒙古舰队还没有到日本的时候，海上就括起大风把许多船沉没了。剩下的船到了日本的海岸就被日本舰队打败了。忽必烈三次预备舰队去打日本；三次都失败了。到了这个地步，他才放弃了打日本的计划，只管国内的事情了。

　　忽必烈有一样的好处：他虽然自己不是文人，他可看得出来中国的文化是非常好的，是蒙古人所应当得的。他就请了宋朝的文人帮他的忙。大多数的文人不肯给一个鞑子做事；少数的文人以为这是施行文化侵略的一个好机会。他们作的文章不都是照着古时候的模范来写的。所以元朝的时候出了些个新式的文章。最有名的两种是戏曲跟小说。这两种也是现在中国文人最主张的。元朝最有名的一个小说叫「三国志演义」。这个小说说的是诸葛亮跟曹操那些人的事情。我们以前讲的诸葛亮借箭的故事，就是从这部书里来的。

Grand Canal
Routes of Marco Polo
Expeditions against Japan
Route to Java – 1292·93
Voyages under Cheng Ho
(Early Ming period) – 1405·1433

THE MONGOL EMPIRE
(LATE 13TH CENTURY)

第二十一章　东西来往

元朝在中国历史上的地位不算很大的，年代又短。中国人当然也不喜欢在这些半开化的鞑子的手下。可是在世界历史上，蒙古帝国是很要紧的。以前没有这么大的国家。以前亚洲，欧洲，两洲没有在一个人的手下。以前这两洲的来往很少，因为交通非常不方便。

蒙古帝国建立以后，中西的交通比前代更便利了。那时候从东边到西边的陆路有南北两条：一条是由天山北路出西伯利亚经过俄国；一条是由天山南路出中亚洲经过阿拉伯到欧洲。窝阔台的时候在这大道上每隔几十里设一个站，站上有给人跟马预备的吃的喝的。所以蒙古人对于传达命令跟商旅的往来一点儿阻碍没有。至于海道，从中国的沿海各地方经过印度洋到波斯湾也很方便。又在上海，杭州，宁波，广州等地方设立专管水路通商的机关。

东方文化的西去

蒙古人开了中西交通的大道，中国跟希腊罗马的文明就直接发生关系了。中国的物质文明对于世界最有影响的要算「磁针」「火药」和「印刷术」。这三种就是在元朝的时候传到欧洲的。

西方文化的东来

蒙古人最喜欢「工艺」和「科学」。他们很优待外国人，所以波斯，阿拉伯，义国跟法国的学者跟美术家都到中国来了。

最有名的西国旅行家是马可波罗，一个义国人。他在中国住了二十年。忽必烈很喜欢他，派他作扬州的大官。你们记得在第五世纪有一个中国和尚名叫法显，走到印度，在路上作了一本记录。第十三世纪的这位马可波罗也写了一本书，就是「马可波罗旅行记」，述说了蒙古帝国里的生活。

元朝灭亡

虽然忽必烈，还有些个很开化的蒙古人，用心学中国的文化，大多数的蒙古人还是不行。所以过了一百五十多年，蒙古人过的还是游牧生活不是城市生活。中国的文化他还是不能领受。在一千三百六十八年有一个做过和尚的朱元璋起了革命，把蒙古人都赶出万里长城去了。中国的主权跟领土又恢复了。

第二十二章　明　朝

蒙古人虐待中国人

蒙古自从统一了中国以后，就把中国的人分成四个阶级。第一个阶级自然是蒙古人。第二是色目人西藏的藏人跟新疆的回人，一共三十一种都包括在内。第三是汉人，那就是蒙古打平了金朝的时候，所得的契丹人跟满州人还有黄河流域的汉人。最末的是南人，这是指着宋朝灭亡以后在长江流域的汉族人民。这四个阶级，非常的不平等。他们统治大帝国的办法，不外是压迫政策。他们尽力的压迫后两个阶级的人，尤其是南人，不叫他们在政治方面活动，也不准他们作大官，也不许他们使用兵器。十家里头要有一个蒙古人管理他们。元朝末年的政治已经坏到了极点。再加上连年闹灾荒，所以中国有思想的人就趁着这个机会都造起反来了。

明太祖的统一

元朝末年的情形本来跟秦朝末年的情形和隋朝末年的情形没有什么分别，所不同的就是在元朝的时候汉族没有权力。起来革命的不过是些平民。在那些位革命的里头有一位名叫朱元璋的起来了。他先平定了中国的南部。在一千三百六十八年，他在南京作了皇帝，派兵去打元朝。不到一年，就把元朝推翻了。以后他又接着把四川，云南收回来，明朝的统一才算完成

了。在中国历史上由平民起来作天子的除了汉高祖以外就是明
太祖了。

明朝的政治

　　无论是汉人或是外族的人来作中国的皇帝，他们有一个共
同的心理，就是害怕别人来抢他们的皇帝地位。换过一次朝代，
那防备人民活动的方法就严一次。就这么一朝比一朝严，到了
朱元璋作了皇帝，君权算是高到极点了。他有一个弱点，就是
他的疑心太大。他老疑惑别人要造反。在一千三百八十年他把
宰相取消了，把权力完全集中到他一个人身上。他把他的二十
四儿子派到各重要的地方去做王，又复兴起来周朝的封建制度。
他想从此以后中国的皇帝总是姓朱的了。

明成祖

　　明太祖死了以后，他的孙子惠帝作了皇帝。他恐怕他的叔
叔们的权力太大，将来不容易管，就想把他们的王位都取消。
那时候在北平的王是太祖第四个儿子，人都称他燕王。他得了
这个消息就起兵推翻了南京政府，自己作了皇帝。这就是明成
祖年号永乐在一千四百二十一年他把政府从南京搬到北京。永
乐年是明朝最强盛的时代。他不但把满州蒙古跟安南打服了，
并且派一个宦官名叫郑和的到南洋各国去，叫各国到中国来进
贡。他这样的重用宦官就是因为宦官在他打南京的时候很帮他

的忙，报告他很多秘密的消息。所以以后明朝所有的皇帝都相信宦官，也就是因为这个缘故。这个正如同明太祖当过几天和尚所以明朝的庙也特别的多。你们可以到北平的各地方去参观参观，差不多每一个胡同儿里就有一个庙。

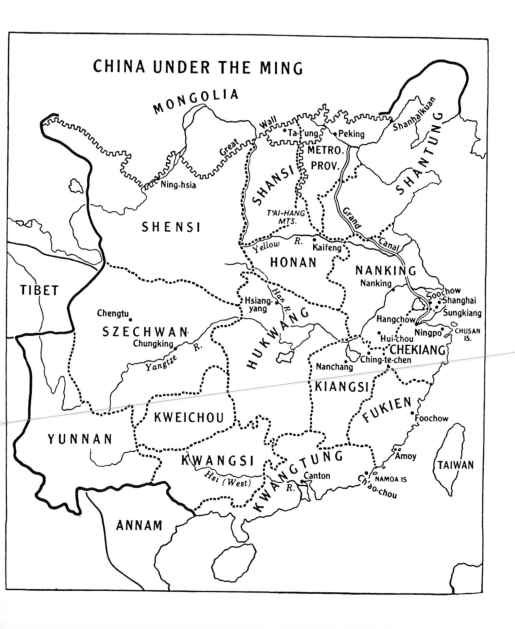

CHINA UNDER THE MING

第二十三章　明朝的外交

郑和下西洋

郑和出使到各国去，自然不只是西洋。可是在中国历史上说惯了，总是说：「下西洋」所以我们这里用的题目也是用「下西洋」三个字。明成祖打破南京的时候，皇宫里起了大火，惠帝也不见了。有人说他跑到外国去了，所以成祖很不放心，就派郑和到各国去。一方面是叫各国到中国来进贡，一方面打听惠帝的下落。现在我们先说一说郑和的历史。

郑和他本来姓马，是回教人。老家在西域，后来搬到云南去了。他的祖先曾有人到过南洋，所以他的航海的知识很多。他也能说当时在南洋一带通用的阿拉伯话。后来进皇宫去做了宦官。在一千四百○五年他第一次出使到外国去。成祖给他造了大船六十二只，长四十四丈，宽十八丈。又叫他带着二万七千八百多兵，从苏州起身，又经过福建就出洋了。郑和每到一个国宣传中国政府怎么好，怎么强；然后服从的就赏给他们金银，不服从的就用武力打他们。他从一千四百○五年到一千四百三十三年一共出国七次。他在海上的生活足有三十年。他到过三十多个国家。他去的地方有安南，暹罗，马来半岛，苏门答腊、爪哇，婆罗洲，印度，阿拉伯跟非洲东岸的马达加斯加岛。

明朝跟日本的关系

日本自从跟元朝打仗以后，就禁止他们的人民和中国往来。很多做海上买卖的人没有事情可做，就都跑到海上去做强盗了。他们常常到中国沿海的各地方来捣乱。明成祖作皇帝的时候日本派人来给他贺喜。他就封日本的大将足利义满做日本的国王。足利义满把海盗的领袖拿住了，送到中国；可是成祖也没定他的罪就叫他们把他带回去了。在一千五百五十年左右浙江一带的海盗闹得更厉害了。沿海的人民管日本的海盗叫蝴蝶儿兵，因为他们的衣裳又肥又大，跑起来好象蝴蝶儿飞的一样。那时候有两位有名的大将：一叫俞大猷，一位叫戚继光跟他们打了十几年才把他们打平了。

日本的海盗平定了不久，中日在朝鲜的战争就起来了。在一千五百九十二年，日本的大将丰臣秀吉想先把朝鲜灭了，再去侵略明朝，所以就发兵攻打朝鲜。可惜朝鲜不是日本的敌手，打了没有多少日子，朝鲜的京城，就被日本打下来了。因为那时候的朝鲜是中国的属国，所以不能袖手旁观，也就加入战争了。这次的战争一共打了七年，才把已经丢了的地方得回来。

明朝跟西洋的关系

在一千五百十七年葡萄牙人到广东来做买卖。他们就住在广州附近的澳门。有几次明朝借用他们的兵船打海盗。他们就

借着这个题目，向明朝的政府要求把澳门租给他们。明朝虽然不愿意，也没有法子。就在一千五百五十七年答应了他们的要求。说好了每年的租银是五百两。这是中国有外国租界的起始。从此以后西班牙人，荷兰人和英国人都陆续的到中国做买卖来了。

在一千五百八十二年天主教徒利玛窦也到广东来了。一千六百年到了北京，把基督圣母图跟许多的土物献给皇帝。皇帝也特别的优待他，也准他在城里头设立教堂。当时的大臣们都喜欢跟他交朋友，并且跟他学了天文，几何，测量等等的学问。中国人看了他的地图，才知道世界有五大洲。西洋科学传到中国，可以说是由他介绍的。

还有一位很有名的荷兰国教徒汤若望也在明朝末个皇帝崇祯的时候（一千六百二十八至一千六百四十三）到北京来了。他给中国改正了历法。他又给明朝造了十二门大炮打满洲兵。到了清朝康熙的时候，还是用他管理历法的事情。

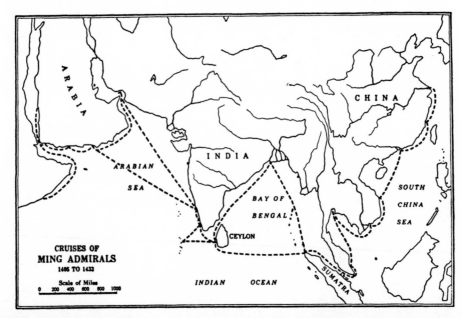

第二十四章　明朝的思想

大哲学家王阳明

明朝的学术思想还是宋朝的那一套，没有什么出奇的。可是其中有一位最有名的大哲学家就是王阳明先生。他最重要的学说，就是「知行合一」。「知」就是知道的「知」，「行」就是做的意思。他说：「知是行的开始，行是知的完成。知跟行是一个整个儿的，不可分为两个事情。他又说了一个比方来解释这个意思，他说：「看好看的，是「知」的一方面；喜欢好看的，是「行」的一方面。人看好看的时候，心里已经喜欢他了；不是看见好看的以后，再去喜欢他」。又说：「人知道他冷的时候，他已经冷了。知道饿的时候，他已经饿了。所以一说「知」，里头已经有「行」了；一说「行」，里头一定有「知」：是不能分开的。」

王阳明这种学说也是从中国的一部古书—书经—里的：「知道不难，实行很难」一句话研究出来的。目的是要人注意行，所以把行说的很难。孙中山先生看这些意思都跟现代中国的情形不合，他就发明了「知难行易」的学说。并且说了许多的比方来证明他的学说是对的。现在我说他的一个很有趣的比方给你们听一听：在某一个大工厂里，有一天全部的机器也不知道为什么都停止了。厂长急的了不得。他赶紧把工人找来叫他们

75

看是什么毛病，可是他们谁也没看出来。正在这个时候，来了一个老工头。他把全部的机器细细儿的看了一回。末后他找到了一个地方，就拿起家伙来照着那个地方打了一下子，全部的机器又呼咙呼咙的活动起来了。厂长自然是很喜欢，就问那个老工头要多少钱。他说：「您给拿一百块钱吧」。厂长很奇怪的问他说：「你来并没费什么事，不过就打了一下子。为什么要那么些钱」。他说：我要的钱不多，我打这一下子不过值一块钱。可是你要知道，在什么地方打这一下子，是值九十九块钱的。

明朝的灭亡

明朝除了开国的两个皇帝以外，其余的皇帝都不喜欢管国事。他们都相信宦官。把政府的大权都交在宦官手里。那些宦官都是些个没有什么学问的人。他们就知道要钱，所以明朝的政治糟的不能问了。崇祯本来是一个很要强的皇帝。可是当他做皇帝的那一年，就赶上陕西闹饥荒。各省的人民也都因为受不了政府的压迫，就都起来造反了。这些个造反的里头有一个叫李自成的，在一千六百四十三那一年，打进了北京。崇祯皇帝就在煤山上自杀了。那时候明朝有一个大将，叫吴三桂，请来了满洲兵，才把李自成赶跑了。以后还有三个王先后在南京，福州跟广东做了十几年的皇帝。到了一千六百六十二年，就被清朝给灭了。

第二十五章　清　朝

满洲的兴起

满洲是中华民族的一个重要份子。他们跟侵略宋朝的金国是一族的人。到了明末的时候才叫满洲，所以清太祖努尔哈赤在一千六百十六年做皇帝的时候，国号也叫金。历史家都称他是后金。到了他儿子清太宗的时候，势力更大了。他先统一了东北，又平定了内蒙古，打败了朝鲜。在一千六百三十六年把国号改为清。满洲这两个字就做了他们种族的名字了。在一千六百四十四那一年。太宗的儿子顺治把京城从沈阳搬到北京。就做了中国的皇帝。

清朝初期的政治

满清不过是东北一部分少数的民族。他们能在中国做了二百多年的皇帝，也有相当的理由。本来满人受中国文化的影响很深，对于中国风俗习惯都很熟悉。对于汉人的思想也很明白。所以统一全国以后，在政治上收到很大效果。他们的眼光远，方法也很好。满人要打算得一个地方不去直接的占领，他们利用明朝投降的将官去攻打或是劝他们服从清朝。他们完全尊重中国的文化。对于明朝的旧制度仍然是保存着。满人又特别的童看学术，优待文人。因为这个缘故，所以清初的学术很发达。

他们想出种种的方法来笼络知识份子。笼络不成，就用很利害
的手段压迫他们。现在把满人的政策分三部分来说：

一、满人进关以后，所用的是笼络政策。一切的行政差不
   多是顺从人民的意思。他们知道人民都想明朝，所以
   极力的保护十三陵。知道人民纳的税很重，就减少了
   他们的钱粮。凡是从前不平等的制度也都取消了。

二、满人也知道知识份子在社会上占重要的地位。进关以
   后又优待他们。清初的时候很有几位有名的学者，康
   熙请他们出来做官。但是他们都不肯。政府也就随他
   们的意思不压迫他们。同时叫各省保举品行跟学问都
   好的人，到北京来做政府的顾问。康熙、雍正、乾隆
   三朝为提倡学术。在各地设立书局。又做了很多有价
   值的书，象康熙字典，古今图书集成跟四库全书都是
   最有名的。

三、满人的笼络政策得了很大的功效。然而也有不少的有
   志气的学者不受满人的笼络。对于满清政府到底是抱
   着反抗的态度。满人为压制这种反动的思想和言论，
   就把很多的学者杀了。清政府也明知道这些被杀的人
   里头一定有错杀的，可是为了要压制反抗的言论，就
   不得不这么办。

清朝的武功

清朝的武功在中国历史上除了元朝以外，可以说是第一。

汉朝唐朝的武功虽然很盛，但是结果都不能长久。满清政府一面发展领土，一面融合各地的民族。在那个时候，中国的国界就定好了。清朝的武功也是康熙，雍正跟乾隆三朝最盛。他们先后平定了外蒙古，天山南北路，西藏和青海，中国的苗族，缅甸，安南，尼泊尔和琉球。这三朝远征的结果，融合了汉，满，蒙，回，藏，苗六大民族。中华民族从此团结成为一个大团体。

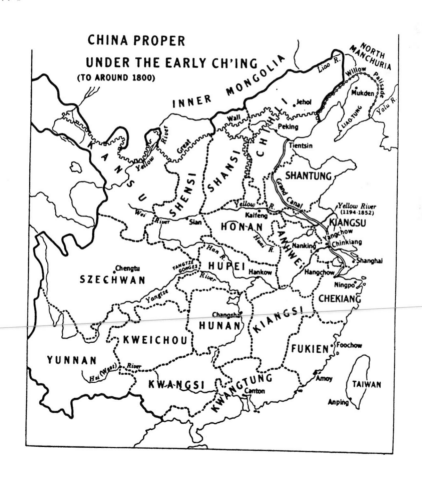

CHINA PROPER
UNDER THE EARLY CH'ING
(TO AROUND 1800)

第二十六章　清朝与西洋的外交

鸦片战争

鸦片战争是中国近代史上一件大事。因为这次的战争，不但使中国的政治、经济，社会连思想各方面都起了很大的变化。而且使中国独立、自由和领土主权也受了很大的打击。从此以后国内和国外许多不幸的事情就接连着来了。满清政府也就发生摇动了。

鸦片战争到底是怎么起的呢？这里面有历史的背景和国际的关系。第一是中外思想的冲突。在鸦片战争以前中外的思想完全不同。在那个时候中国是东方第一的大国。国家的力量最强，文化也最高。那些邻近的小国都尊敬中国，看中国是一个最上的国。他们看自己是中国的属国。所以那时候东方的国际关系，是上国跟属国的关系。同时在西方的国家本来是互相侵略。等到航海成功以后，所遇见的只是美洲跟非洲的土人。他们的知识和文化程度都相当的低，所以航海的人都有侵略的野心。到东亚来的西国人也免不了有这种思想。可是中国仍然以为自己是大国，把他们当作属国，所以就发生冲突了。

第二是通商的问题。自从乾隆以来，中国跟外国通商只能在广州一个地方，而且必须经过一定的手续。英国人对于这些限制都觉着不方便。好几次要求更改通商的办法，但是都没有成功，所以中外的感情就越来越坏了。

　　以上所说的两点是战争的远因，鸦片不过是这次战争的一个最近的原因。那时候清政府派林则徐为钦差大臣，到广州去负责办理禁烟的事情。他办事是很认真的。他说：「鸦片不赶紧禁止，那么国家就越来越穷，人民就越来越弱。再过几十年，不但是没有可筹的款，并且也没有可练的兵了」。战争的结果，中国败了。就在南京订立了条约，要点是：

一、开广州，厦门，福州，宁波，上海等五口通商。

二、把香港给英国。

三、赔款二千一百万两，分四年交清。

四、两国往来的公文要平等。

五、按照公平的法子定新的税法。外国货在一个口纳税以后，就可以运到内地去，不用再纳税了。

六、从前的商行也叫公行都取消。

　　第二年虎门又订了一个条约，把南京条约不清楚的地方又解释一下子。要紧的有四点：

一、进口税是「值百抽五」。

二、领事裁判权。

三、最惠国。

四、通商的章程。

第二十七章 外交的结果

太平天国

太平天国是农民发起的一种社会革命运动，这次的革命运动是政治腐败的结果。清朝到了乾隆末年和嘉庆的时候，无论是社会政治和经济，各方面都到了极危险的地步。按着清政府的计算，中国在康熙四十年（一千七百〇一）人口大约有一万两千万（120,000,000）到了嘉庆五年（一千八百）人口增加到三万万（300,000,000）一百年之内增加一倍多。人口既是增加了，不知道利用科学的方法增加生产，那么人民的生计发生了很大的问题。再加上每年的天灾，政治的腐败和外国的侵略，就造成了太平天国的革命运动。

太平天国的领袖是洪秀全，他是广西的农民。他到广州去考过两次，都没考上。他在广州的时候入了耶稣教信仰上帝，创立了「上帝会」。称上帝是「天父」，耶稣是「天兄」他是「天弟」。凡是入教的男的称弟兄，女的称姐妹，都平等。他明着宣传宗教，暗着反对清朝。恰巧那时候，广西连年闹饥荒，穷苦的农民都加入了「上帝会」。没有多少日子，他就建立了太平天国。在一千八百五十三年占领了南京，就定为国都。他们的政治可以分做四个要点：

一、施行公田，公产制度：分天下的田地为九等。不论男女都有分得田地的机会。不许私自藏金银。有饭大家吃，有钱大家用。这是他们的经济政策。

二、提倡男女平等：他们主张一夫一妻。不许买卖人口。
　　禁止妇女缠足。政府也要设立女官。男女同等考试。
　　地位完全平等。

三、宣传宗教：他们在各处设立教堂，宣传宗教，规定读
　　圣经和早晚礼拜为日常生活。借着宣传的力量，增进
　　人民的信仰，完成革命的工作。

四、改良风俗习惯：绝对禁止鸦片和赌钱，不准喝酒。

太平天国跟清朝打了有十几年的仗，占了有十六省的地盘。
到了后来，做大官的都讲究奢侈的生活，内部起了纷争，情形
就越来越坏了。清朝的大将曾国藩，李鸿章等联合起来，慢慢
的就把太平天国灭了。

英法联军

南京条约成立以后，福州，厦门，上海，宁波四口都开了。
就是广州的人民很利害，不许英国人进城。中国的官又在英国
的船上拿去了几个中国的水手，并且把英国的国旗也拔下来了。
正在这个时候，中国人民又在广西杀死了几个法国的传教士。
法国就借着这件事跟英国军队联合起来，打进了广州，要求清
朝改订通商条约。美国跟俄国也提出了同样的要求，但是都没
有结果。英法联军打到了天津。清政府没有法子就订立了天津
条约，要点是：

一、除了南京条约的五口以外，又准许英法商人在牛庄，
　　芝罘，台湾，汕头，海南岛等地方做买卖。

二、在北京设立使馆。　　　　五、自由传道。

三、随便在内地旅行。　　　　六、鸦片公卖。

四、在各重要的地方设立领事馆。　七、准许移民。

天津条约签字以后，第二年到北京来换约。没想到在半道儿上又起了麻烦。一千八百六十年英法联军打进了北京，烧了圆明园，那时候俄国公使出来说和。除了订好了的天津条约以外，又订立了北京条约。要紧的三件是：

一、九龙半岛的一部分给英国。

二、天津也做为通商的地方。

三、赔军费八百万两。

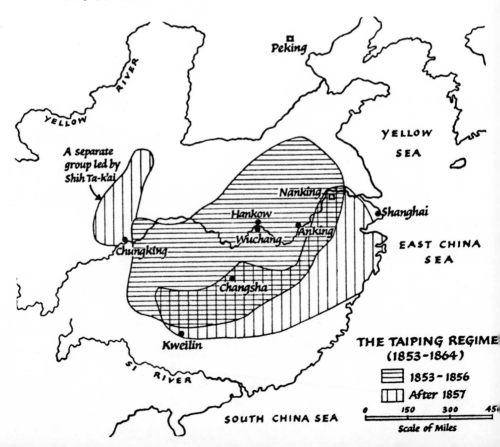

THE TAIPING REGIME
(1853-1864)

1853-1856

After 1857

第二十八章　清朝的末年

中日战争

日本自从「明治维新」以后，向外发展的政策分南进北进两条道路。南进的桥梁是台湾，目的在南洋。北进的桥梁是朝鲜，目的在大陆。要打通这两条道路，必得先侵略中国。那时候朝鲜的政府是软弱无能的。社会上有一个党。叫「东学党」意思是研究东方的学问。他们打着救国的旗子，聚集了好几千人，反对政府。朝鲜的政府管不了他们，就求中国帮助。清政府立刻就派兵到朝鲜去了。日本借着保护侨民，也就进兵了。等到乱事平定以后，中国又叫日本退兵。日本不听，反到要求中国共同改革朝鲜的政治，并且强迫朝鲜政府宣言，废除中国跟朝鲜的一切条略。中国不能同意。

在交涉很紧急的时候，中国的大臣大部分都主战，只有李鸿章知道这仗开不得，希望和平解决。谁知道日本故意的找毛病，忽然攻击中国军舰。清政府不能再忍，不得已就跟日本宣战了。

这一次的战争是中国近一百年来第二次的重大打击。战争以后，外国的报纸评论说：日本不是跟中国打仗，实在是跟李鸿章打仗。这话说的太过，倒是也有相当的理由。因为那时候，各省都是保护自己，谁也不管谁。就是要说要派兵帮助的，那

也不过是一句空话。最可笑的是有一只军舰被日本拿去了，管海军的官要求日本把那一只军舰放了，说那一只军舰是广东的。这一次的战争跟广东没有关系。这真是一个笑话。假使日本真是跟李鸿章一个人开仗，那么李鸿章虽然是败了也是很光荣的。

维新运动

清朝的「维新运动」是中国近代史上的一件大事。这一种运动是少数有眼光的知识份子看到了中国的旧法不能抵抗外国的侵略，所以就主张学西洋文化。这一种运动可以分两个时期。第一个时期注意的是模仿西洋的物质科学。第二个时期注意的是改革政治，文化。现在把以上的两点再说一说。

鸦片战争以后，中国有知识的人，都知道非学西洋不可。李鸿章自然是这些人的代表。因为他跟外国人的交际很多，认识西洋文化也比较深。他做事有决断。北洋的海军和陆军都是他创办的。他还开办了许多的工业。等到「中日战争」以后，「维新运动」又转到另一个方向了。

「中日战争」停止了，多年训练的北洋舰队完全失败了。从此以后，国民又受了很大的刺激。知道靠着军舰，大炮，还是不能够救中国。他们觉得必得从政治方面改革才能有办法。所以康有为，梁起超的「变法运动」就起来了。

他们的新法对于教育，实业，军事和政治都有重要的改革。

这次的变法是少数有思想的人极力的提倡，由光绪皇帝下命令实行的。可是当时的政权不在光绪手里，是在西太后手里。西太后是守旧的，反对新法，所以这「维新运动」到底是失败了。

义和团和八国联军

在维新运动的时期，外国人很赞成新党。政变以后，康梁都跑到外国去，外国人也保护他们。因为这个缘故，西太后跟旧党很恨外国人。西太后想把光绪废了，由皇族里挑出一个人来做皇帝。外国也都不赞成。西太后的排外思想就越来越厉害了。这时候山东的义和团起来了。他们的口号是「保护清朝灭洋人」。旧党想利用这些义和团排外，所以这从来没有的大乱就发生了。

义和团是白莲教的一派，是有宗教性质的一种秘密会。他们自己说：能请神，并且不怕枪炮。起初是在山东，后来被袁世凯给赶到河北省来了。清政府的一般大臣们都很相信他们，崇拜他们。让他们随便做事。他们进了北京以后，闹的就更厉害了。他们拆铁路，毁电线，杀教士，烧教堂，无所不为。后来日本使馆的书记和德国公使，先后叫他们给杀了。清政府不明白利害，就在一千九百年下命令跟各国宣战。这才惹的「八国联军」打进了北京。西太后跟光绪皇帝跑到西安去了。清政府又派李鸿章为全权大臣跟联军议和。又订了一个不平等条约才算完事。李鸿章也就在第二年（一千九百〇一）死了。

　　八国联军以后，西太后所受的打击更大了。她把光绪以前所行的新法都慢慢的施行出来。可是还不能叫人民满意。日俄战争以后，人民看日本是立宪国胜了，俄国是专制国败了，所以人民就要求政府立宪了。清政府不得已就派了五个大臣出洋考察政治，做一个立宪的准备。其实清政府不过是为敷衍人民，免得他们起革命，心里就没有诚意立宪。西太后跟光绪不久都死了，溥仪做了皇帝。清政府把军政的大权完全集中在皇族的手里。把进京请愿的代表也赶走了。人民所希望的立宪还是不能实现。一千九百一十一年十月十日民军在武昌起了革命，没有多少日子，各省都响应了。孙中山先生就在一千九百十二年一月一日，做了中华民国临时的大总统，到了本年的二月，溥仪就退位了。

China during the late 19th and early 20th centuries, showing the treaty ports, leased territories, and areas of Taiping and Boxer control. (3)

Chronological Table

The Hsia Kingdom (traditional?)	*ca.* 1994 B.C.–*ca.* 1523
The Shang (or Yin) Kingdom	*ca.* 1523 B.C.–*ca.* 1028
The Chou Kingdom	*ca.* 1027 B.C.–256
The Ch'in dynasty	221 B.C.–207
The Western (or Earlier) Han dynasty	202 B.C.–A.D. 9
The Hsin dynasty	A.D. 9–A.D. 23
The Eastern (or Later) Han dynasty	25– 220
The Three Kingdoms	220– 265
Shu, 221–264	
Wei, 220–265	
Wu, 222–280	
The Western Tsin dynasty	265– 317
The Eastern Tsin dynasty	317– 420
The Former (or Liu) Sung dynasty	420– 479
The Southern Ch'i dynasty	479– 502
The Southern Liang dynasty	502– 557
The Southern Ch'ên dynasty	557– 589
The Northern Wei dynasty	386– 535
The Eastern Wei dynasty	534– 550
The Western Wei dynasty	535– 556
The Northern Ch'i dynasty	550– 577
The Northern Chou dynasty	557– 581
The Later Liang dynasty	555– 587
The Sui dynasty	590– 618
The T'ang dynasty	618– 906
The Five dynasties	907– 960
Later Liang, 907–923	
Later T'ang, 923–936	
Later Chin, 936–947	
Later Han, 947–950	
Later Chou, 951–960	
The Liao dynasty	907– 1125
The Northern Sung dynasty	960– 1126
The Hsi-hsia dynasty	990– 1227
The Southern Sung dynasty	1127– 1279
The Chin dynasty	1115– 1234
The Yüan dynasty	1260– 1368
The Ming dynasty	1368– 1644
The Ch'ing dynasty	1644– 1912
The Republic	1912–

CHINA'S CENTURY OF UNEQUAL TREATIES

WORLD EVENTS   **YEAR**   **CHINA'S TREATIES**   **JAPAN**

1830

1834 BRITISH EAST INDIA CO
monopoly ended.

1834 Lord Napier's Mission
1836 Capt. Elliott's Mission

TAO KUANG

1840 "Opium War"

1842 *TREATY or NANKING*
1843 *TREATY of THE BOGUE*
1844 *TREATY of WANGHSIA*

TRADE TREATIES
1844 France
1845 Belgium
1847 Sweden & Norway
1851 Russia

BRITAIN
1. Ports opened: Canton, Amoy,
   Foochow, Shanghai, Ningpo
2. Diplomatic equality
3. Fixed tariff
4. Indemnity for destroyed
   opium, cohong debt, war
   expense.
5. Hong Kong ceded to Britain
6. Cohongs abolished

BRITAIN
1. Tariff scheduled at 5%
2. Extraterritoriality
3. Most favored nation clause
4. Trade regulations

U.S.
1. Diplomatic equality
2. Extraterritoriality
3. Right to employ Chinese
4. Opium recognized as
   contraband
5. Review at end of 12 years

1853 Perry visits Japan

1850

1852 Britain occupies Pegu
1854 CRIMEAN WAR

1854 *SHANGHAI SETTLEMENT*

1856 "Arrow War"

1857 Indian Mutiny
1858 India transferred to the
Crown

1858 *TIENTSIN TREATIES*
1859 Expedition to Peking
1860 *PEKING TREATIES*

1861 Foreign Office created

BASIC BRITISH TREATY
1. Kowloon ceded
2. Ports opened: 6 coastal,
   5 river ports
3. Legations at Peking
4. Travel in interior
5. Consuls
6. Tolerance for Christianity
7. Opium legalized, taxed
8. Emigration permitted

EDICTS OF RELIGIOUS TOLERANCE
1844 ->
1. Chinese permitted to become Christians
2. Permission to erect churches
3. Restoration of Roman Catholic churches
   destroyed during previous 150 years.

Imperial Maritime
Customs established
with foreign officers

FRANCE
1. Reparations for
   land confiscated
   from Christians
2. Missionaries
   permitted to secure
   land anywhere

RUSSIA
1. Right of cor-
   respondence
   between Min-
   isters of state
2. Promorsk

HSIEN FENG

Taiping
Rebellion

1860

1861 U.S. CIVIL WAR
1863 France occupies Cochin
and Cambodia.

T'UNG CHIH

1868 MEIJI

U.S.
1. Most favored
   nation
   treatment

1869 Suez Canal opened
1870 FRANCO-PRUSSIAN WAR

1870

1868 Burlingame Mission

JAPAN
1. Reciprocal extra territor-
   iality in ports only
2. Diplomatic intercourse

1871 Treaty with China

1874 Formosa expedition

1875
1876 Treaty with Korea

1880

1876 *CHEFOO CONVENTION*
1877 First Chinese Legation - London

BRITAIN
1. Margary Case
2. Yunnan open to trade
3. Additional ports
4. Tibetan expedition

1882 Legation at Seoul

1882 U.S. Chinese Exclusion Act

1880 *IMMIGRATION TREATY* — U.S. limits but does not prohibit
1881 *TREATY OF ST. PETERSBURG* — Russia retrocedes Ili

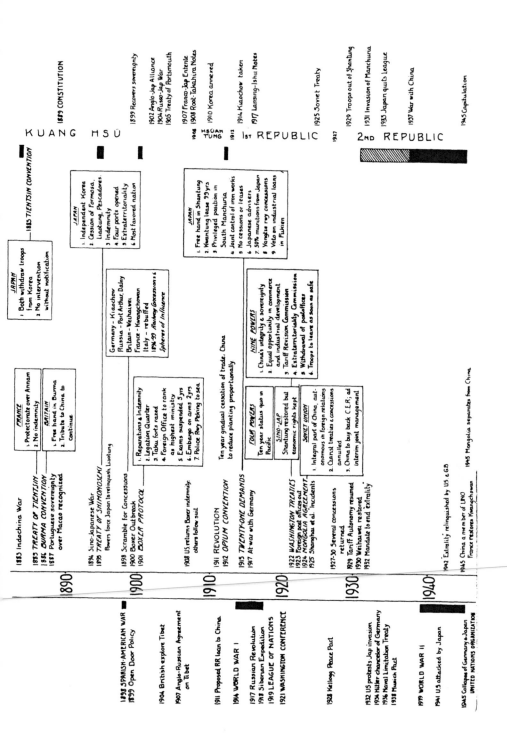

CHAPTER 1 - THE ESTABLISHMENT OF CHINA

Sentences for translation into Chinese

1. The cradle of Chinese civilization was on both
   sides of the lower course of the Yellow River.
2. At that time there were no Chinese in the Yangtze
   River Valley, only half civilized people.
3. Life in those times was much simpler than nowa-
   days.
4. The span (age) of English history is not as long
   as that of Chinese history.
5. You know, of course, that the Xià Dynasty was no
   more than a small city and a little surrounding
   territory.
6. At the time of the Xià Dynasty, the civilization
   of Egypt (Āijígwó) was far more advanced than
   that of China, for the Egyptians had already
   discovered bronze.
7. China did not discover bronze until about the
   6th century B.C.
8. Four thousand years ago, except for the state of
   Xià, there were no civilized peoples in China.
9. Even when you dig very ancient implements out
   of the ground, they aren't sure to be genuine.
10. When the Xià people built houses they always
    built them in the trees or else dug pits in the
    ground.

Classroom Activities

1. Map Talk - Using a wall map of China, give the
   class a brief map talk on "The Cradle of Chinese
   Civilization".
2. Comparative History Talk - From your general
   knowledge of the history of the western world,
   tell a Chinese friend briefly what was going on
   in the occident during the Xià and Shāng times
   in China.

CHAPTER 2 - THE SHĀNG DYNASTY

Sentences for translation into Chinese

1. Before the discovery of bronze, man's tools were
   made of stone or bone.
2. In the Stone Age men built huts in the trees to
   escape the wild animals.
3. The Shāng State originally was in Shānsyī province,
   but it later assimilated many neighboring states.
4. The Shāng territory grew bigger and bigger.
5. If we look at the tools dug up at Ānyáng, we can
   know how the people of those times lived.
6. Many Shāng Dynasty things are still extant.
7. Some historians say that the Shāng Dynasty was
   extinguished in the 12th century; others say that
   it was not extinguished until the middle of the
   11th century.
8. Among the animals domesticated by man were the
   dog, the pig, the ox and the horse.
9. Writing probably was invented in the Shāng period.
   The characters engraved on bones were very simple
   and quite unlike the characters that are written
   today.
10. When the Shāng Dynasty decided to escape the
    incursions of the northwestern nomads, they moved
    several hundred lǐ east and built a new city in
    northern Honan province which they called Ānyáng.

Classroom Activities

1. Map Talk - show the geographical relation of Xià
   and Shāng and the location of the new Shāng city
   of Ānyáng.
2. Talk briefly on the progress of civilization
   during the second millenium B.C. in the Yellow
   River Valley.

CHAPTER 3 - THE ZHŌU DYNASTY

Sentences for translation into Chinese

1. People may ask why Chinese dynasties moved their
   capitals from one place to another.
2. The Zhōu Dynasty may be divided into three periods, of 200-250 years each.
3. At the outset the Zhōu kings were very strong;
   in the second period their powers became less
   and less; in the last period they had no power
   at all.
4. At the beginning of the Period of the Warring
   States there were 770 little states all at war
   with each other.
5. In the end there were only seven states left
   because the rest had all been wiped out.
6. After defeating Chǔ, the King of Chǐn unified
   all of China Proper except two places: one the
   southeast coastal region, the other the mountain
   regions of the southwest.
7. Before the invention of bronze coins people
   bartered goods, so when they first made coins
   they made them in the shape of knives or bells.
8. The mule is a better beast of burden than the
   horse because the horse is less tractable than
   the mule.
9. Every period of Chinese History has had floods
   and droughts, so the Chinese people very early
   learned to store grain in granaries for sale in
   bad years.
10. Iron was discovered probably in the Zhōu
    Period, but we can't say that people immediately
    made all of their tools of iron; at the outset
    only weapons were made of iron, while the tools
    of the common people were still made of wood
    and stone and bones.

Classroom Activities

1. Map and Chart Talk - Trace the spread of Chinese
   culture during the first three dynasties, pointing out the locations of such states as have
   been mentioned in the test.

CHAPTER 4 - THE PHILOSOPHERS OF THE ZHŌU DYNASTY

Sentences for translation into Chinese

1. China's greatest contribution to world culture
   is the Confucian philosophy.
2. The teachings of Mòzǐ did not have much influence on Chinese thought.
3. I have here a very difficult problem which I
   should like to have you help me solve.
4. The major differences among the four schools of
   thought lie in their differing methods for
   improving society.
5. Of these four schools of thought there was only
   one which considered man's nature to be originally bad, and that was the School of Law.
6. Confucius did not write many books himself;
   most of his teachings were written down by his
   pupils.
7. Most of the Zhōu Dynasty philosophers were also
   officials of one state or another.
8. Most of the things written in this period belong
   to the three categories of history, philosophy
   and poetry.

Classroom Activities - As a review of the first four
chapters, make brief classroom talks on such topics
as:

1. China's progress in housing and building.

2. The geographical spread of Chinese culture in
   the milleniums B.C.
3. The Three Ages: Stone, Bronze, Iron.
4. The influence of the northwestern nomads on
   early China.
5. Development of writing and the tools of writing.
6. The Beginnings of Chinese Literature.
7. The Period of the Warring States.
8. The influence of geography on the expansion of
   Chinese culture.
9. Progress in tools and weapons.
10. From city state to empire.

CHAPTER 5 - THE TEACHINGS OF THE FOUR SCHOOLS

Sentences for translation into Chinese

1. The writings of Confucius, Mòzǐ, Lǎozǐ and
   Shāng Yāng have all been translated into English.
2. The Teachings of Mòzǐ and the teachings of Jesus
   cannot be said to be identical, but they do have
   a good many similarities.
3. The teaching "All under heaven are one family"
   means that all men are brothers and should not
   make war on each other.
4. The Taoists said that since man's nature is
   naturally good, there was no need to control him
   by means of laws; but the Legalists said that
   since man is by nature bad, you cannot control
   him without laws.
5. If a man wants to rule others he must first learn
   to rule himself--this is a teaching of Confucius.
6. Mencius and Zhuangzǐ developed the teachings of
   the Rú and Dào Schools into orderly systems of
   philosophy.
7. If the teachings of Mòzǐ could be put into
   practice today, perhaps all under Heaven would
   become one family.
8. Both Lǎozǐ and Mòzǐ taught that love can enable
   a man to master (conquer) many difficult problems.

Classroom Activities

1. Memorize and repeat all of the examples of the
   teachings of the Four Schools given in the text.
   Don't fail to get the rhythms produced by
   balanced sentence structure.
2. Chart Talk - Give a brief talk following the
   chart of the Four Schools.

CHAPTER 6 - QÍN UNIFIES CHINA

Sentences for translation into Chinese

1. There were two occasions on which the State of
   Chǔ almost overcame its enemies, but on neither
   occasion did it succeed.
2. Qín Shǐhúang's armies conquered all the way to
   Indo-China on the South.
3. The short walls built during the Period of the
   Warring States were later linked together by the
   State of Qín to form the Great Wall of China.
4. The original territory of the State of Qín lay
   near the Xiōngnú, so they frequently suffered
   from their attacks.
5. So large an area of land required the digging of
   canals and the making of roads before it could
   become a single state.
6. Although Qín wiped out the feudal system and
   allowed the common people to buy land, nevertheless the life of the common people was still very
   bitter because of the work of building the Great
   Wall.
7. Under the feudal system a farmer tilled the
   fields for his lord and received a small portion
   of the crops for his own use.
8. Centralized government means that the local officials were no longer independent but had to obey
   the orders of the Emperor.
9. The Great Wall has a history of 2000 years but

it has been unable to prevent the inroads of
the Tatars.
10. When penalties are harsh, the people obey the
law; when penalties are light, the people do not
fear the law. This is the teaching of the Legalist School.

Classroom Activities

1. Map Talk - Give a brief talk on The Great Wall of
China, using a wall map to indicate its course.
2. Debate - Confucianists generally regard Qín
Shihuǎng as a bad ruler because of his "burning
of books and killing of scholars". Debate the
pros and cons.

CHAPTER 7 - THE HÀN DYNASTY

Sentences for translation into Chinese

1. Some of the Hàn Emperors followed Taoist methods
in their administration of government; others
used the methods of the Confucian School.
2. Wǎng Mǎng wished to change not only the system
of officials of the Han Dynasty but also the
military system and the land system.
3. Most Chinese emperors sprang from the upper
classes, but not the founder of the Hàn Dynasty.
4. The two greatest weaknesses of Chinese emperors
were (i) relying on their empresses' relatives
and (ii) relying on eunuchs.
5. Wǎng Mǎng's ideas were in many respects very
good, but they were not well suited to those
times.
6. The Confucian School and the Taoist School were
gradually transformed from Schools of Philosophy
into religions.
7. Among the emperors of the Han Dynasty, the most
famous was Hàn Wǔdì; none was more able than he.

8. If you compare the Early and Late Hàn periods
   with the Early and Late Zhōu periods, you will
   see one major difference: the rulers of Eastern
   Zhōu on the one hand lacked ability and on the
   other lacked any real power; but not so the
   Eastern Hàn: the first few emperors had power
   and knew how to handle the affairs of state.

Classroom Activities:

1. Map Talk - Give a brief map talk comparing the
   territorial extent of the Zhōu, Qín and Hàn
   dynasties.
2. Talk - Give a brief talk on the Life Span of a
   Dynasty and Causes for its fall.
3. Talk - From what you know of Roman History, make
   a comparison of the Roman Empire and its great
   contemporary the Hàn Empire, pointing out similarities and contrasts.

CHAPTER 8 - THE HÀN REACHES THE WESTERN REGIONS

Sentences for translation into Chinese

1. When Zhāng Qiān visited the Western Regions he
   learned of the existence of the "Heavenly Horse"
   in Fergana.
2. Zhāng Qiān had no more than gotten outside the
   Great Wall before he was seized by the Xiōngnú
   and taken off into Mongolia.
3. Just at the time that Qín was uniting China, the
   Xiōngnú was also creating a state in the territory north of the Great Wall.
4. It was only from the time that the Hàn Dynasty
   opened the Northern and Southern Trade Routes
   that China began to carry on trade with the
   Western Regions.
5. When Zhāng Qiān saw square bamboo in the land of

the Yuèzhī, he thought that it must have come
from Yúnnán via India.

6. Hàn Wǔdì sent him a second time to contact other
states of the Western Regions in the hope of
getting their help.

7. When Chinese dynasties were strong, they usually
were interested in promoting trade with Central
Asia; when they were weak they were unable even
to regulate internal affairs.

8. Bān Chāo probably went a little farther to the
west than did Zhāng Qiān.

9. Zhāng Qiān and Bān Chāo have another point of
difference: most of Zhāng Qiān's journey was
accomplished alone, but Bān Chāo took an army
with him.

10. The Hàn Empire was contemporary with the Roman
Empire, but covered a much larger extent of
territory.

Classroom Activities

1. Talk - Use the family tree of the Bān family as
a guide and give a brief talk on "A Great Family
in Chinese History".

2. Map Talk - Give a brief map talk on the Northern
and Southern Caravan Routes in Hàn Times.

3. Story Telling - Below you will find a more complete story of Zhāng Qiān's mission than is given
in the text. This is in English. Read it
through two or three times to familiarize your-
self with the facts; then tell the story to the
class in your own words.

4. Interpreting - Simulate a situation where a
visitor from the coastal province of Fukien is
invited to talk to a history class in a Peking
school. He wants to tell them the story of
Zhāng Qiān's Mission but his Fukienese won't be
understood by the Peking students and he can't
speak Mandarin. Fortunately he can speak English, so he tells the story in English and one

of the students, whose English is exceptionally
good, interprets sentence by sentence into
Mandarin.

The Story of Zhāng Qiān's Mission.

Zhāng Qiān was one of Hàn Wǔdì's generals whom
the emperor sent to the Western Regions to find
the Yuèzhī people. At that time the Huns were
making trouble for the emperor on the northern
border. The Great Wall, which Qín had built
seventy or eighty years before for the purpose
of keeping out invaders, was not a success.
Wǔdi had to think of other means of opposing the
Huns. He decided that they must be wiped out
completely. But to do this he needed the help
of other enemies of the Huns. So he sent Zhāng
Qiān to make a treaty with the Yuèzhī who lived
in the western part of the present province of
Gānsù.

Zhāng Qīan started out with only one hundred
horsemen. But, he had hardly gotten beyond the
Great Wall when the Huns attacked his band, cap-
tured him, and took him off to their capital,
somewhere in Mongolia. There he lived for years
pretending to have "turned Tatar". All this
time however he was planning how he might accomplish the mission of the emperor. Moreover, he
learned that the Yuèzhī no longer lived in Gānsù.
They had been driven out by the Huns nearly 40
years earlier, and had migrated westward.

Finally he and one companion escaped and continued their journey·westward until they came to
the state of Fergana. There they learned that
the Yuèzhī were now happily situated in the valley of the Oxus River to the south. So they went
on to the new land of the Yuèzhī. There they

stayed for a year, joining the Yuèzhī in some of
their raids on the state of Parthia to the west
of them. They tried to persuade the Yuèzhī to
come back to their old home and help China destroy
the Huns, but the Yuèzhī people had found a better and more peaceful land, and didn't want to
leave it. So finally Zhāng Qiān and his companion started out to return to China.

On the way back they were again seized by the
Huns and forced to stay with them for another
year. Once more escaping, this time with Zhāng's
Hunnish wife and son, they got back to Chángān
and reported to the emperor.

Although Zhāng Qiān did not succeed in the main
purpose of his mission, we cannot say that it
was a failure. He learned many things which were
very helpful to the emperor. Moreover the result
of his report was that Wǔdì sent him back again
to make treaties with other states in the Western
Region. During the next century the Huns were
defeated over and over again and finally driven
out of Mongolia. They migrated to Russia, and
from there, several centuries later, they invaded
Europe and the Roman Empire.

CHAPTER 9 - THE CULTURE OF THE HÀN DYNASTY

Sentences for translation into Chinese

1. Bān Biāo started to write the History of the
   Former Hàn Dynasty but before he finished it,
   he died.
2. His son Bān Gù continued the work, but he also
   was unable to finish it, so his sister Bān Zhāo
   wrote the last part.
3. There is a story that Hàn Míngdì dreamed of a
   golden man flying back and forth in his palace,

which someone told him was the Buddha.

4. The three members of the Bān family merely wrote a History of the Former Hàn Period, but Sī-mǎ Qiān wrote a history of China from the beginning down to the first century B.C.

5. Although the story of the golden man is not authentic, it may show that Buddhism did come into China during the later Hàn Dynasty.

6. The five colors of the first flag of the Chinese Republic represented the five races of Chinese, Manchus, Mongols, Uigurs, and Tibetans.

7. Wāng Mǎng had occupied the throne for only fifteen years when he was overthrown by a member of the Líu family.

8. The work of building the Great Wall was too large to be completed by a single emperor.

9. Foreign students of Chinese culture call Sī-mǎ Qiān, China's foremost historian.

10. We have already spoken of three religions which arose within China proper. In addition there is Buddhism which was transmitted from India.

Classroom Activities

Make an oral report on:

1. Bānjīade míngrén (the famous people in the Bān family).

2. Zhāng Qiānde gōngzùo (the work of Zhāng Qiān).

3. Wáng Mǎng gǎigé shèhùi (Wang Mang reforms society).

4. Fójiào láidào Zhōngguode lìshǐ (the history of Buddhism's coming to China).

5. Zhōu,Hàn, liǎngcháo wénxúe gōngzùo de bǐjiào (a comparison of literature during Zhou and Han).

6. Qían-hòu liǎng-Hàn zài Xīyù de dòngzùo (the activities of the two Han dynasties in the Western Regions).

7. Hàn Cháo húangdìde chángdǔan (an evaluation of the Han Emperors).

8. Zhōngguo lǐngtǔ cóng jìyuánqián dìshíyī shìjì
   dào jìyuán-hòu dìsān shìjì de kuòzhāng (the
   expansion of Chinese territory from the eleventh
   century B.C. to the third century A.D.).
9. Zhōngguo zhéxué gēn zōngjiào de fāzhǎn (the
   development of Chinese philosophy and religion).

Supplementary Vocabulary

xiāngxiàng	SV:	to resemble, be alike
yìyì	N:	meaning, significance
huángcháo	N:	imperial family, dynasty
biànxiàng	N:	change, metamorphosis
niánhào	N:	reign-name, reign-title
guóhào	N:	name for a state

CHAPTER 10 - THE THREE KINGDOMS

Sentences for translation into Chinese

1. The last years of a dynasty are always chaotic
   because the central power is extinguished, while
   the power of each locality gradually grows
   greater.
2. There were three reasons for the fall of the
   dynasty: the emperors were incompetent, the
   officials were quarreling over territory, and
   the people couldn't make a living; in addition,
   the country frequently suffered inroads of the
   Tatars.
3. Such a goal as that is unattainable.
4. How can you accomplish your purpose if you don't
   take advantage of your opportunities?
5. Whatever he does, succeeds.
6. When he was only five years old he became
   emperor.
7. In five campaigns within three years time he
   didn't win a single victory.
8. If the State of Chi could make an alliance with
   the State of Chu, then the whole country would

be at their mercy (would be theirs).
9. The last time he sent an army to attack Song
   State he suffered a serious defeat.
10. As soon as he heard that his older brother had
    been defeated, he followed suit and surrendered.

Classroom Activities

1. Talk - Give a brief talk comparing the Period of
   the Warring States (B.C. 481-221) and the Period
   of the Three Kingdoms (A.D. 220-280). Point out
   similarities and differences.

2. Give a brief summary of the Period of the
   Three Kingdoms.

CHAPTER 11

PERSONALITIES OF THE THREE KINGDOMS PERIOD

Re-telling the Stories in the Text - Instead of
   answering a series of questions on the text,
   let each student tell one or more of the stories
   through without interruption. It may be memor-
   ized in the words of the text, or told freely in
   the student's own words.

Translate the following story from English history
into Chinese:

THE THREE QUESTIONS

The king of a certain country one day thought
of these three questions: What is the most
important time? Who is the most important man?
What is the most important act? He asked every-
one in the kingdom to answer these questions, but
not a single person gave a reply which was fully
satisfying.

Consequently he later went to see a hermit.
This hermit was tilling the field in front of
his door, so the king helped him plant the field.
When noon came, they sat down to rest, and the
king asked the hermit his three questions, re-
peating them three or four times, but the hermit
did not reply.

Suddenly a man came running toward them, his
whole body covered with blood. He ran up to the
king and fell to the ground. The king and the
hermit together bound up the man's wounds, helped
him into the house and made him lie down on the
bed.

The next morning the king got up quite early
and went to see the wounded man. The wounded man
with tears in his eyes said to the king: "Please
forgive me. You killed my younger brother. As I
was coming with intent to do you harm, I was
wounded by your guards and escaped to this place.
If you had not bound up my wounds, I would certainly have died. From now on I want to serve
you. I beg you to forgive me."

When the king heard this, he was very happy
and hastened to tell the hermit about it. The
hermit smiled and said: "This is the answer to
your three questions." The king asked: "How is
that? I don't understand."

The hermit replied: "If you had not helped
me plant my field yesterday, you would not have
escaped danger. If you had not saved the wounded
man, you would not have conciliated an enemy.
Now you know that the most important time is the
present, the most important man the one before
your face, the most important act to treat
people well."

Supplementary Vocabulary

mǒu . . . . SP: a certain
yǐnshì . . . . . N: hermit
shù . . . . V: forgive
wèibīng . . . . . N: guard
táo . . . . V: escape
shìfèng . . . . . V: serve
héjiě . . . . . . V: conciliate

Classroom Activity - Tell other stories from the
  history and legend of western civilization in
  Chinese as if to a ten-year-old Chinese child.

CHAPTER 12

THE JÌN DYNASTY AND
THE NORTHERN AND SOUTHERN DYNASTIES

Sentences for translation into Chinese

1. Several times in Chinese History a dynasty has
   moved its capital from west to east because of
   the growing strength of the barbarians in the
   northwest.
2. The Northern Wèi state was established in the
   Yellow River Valley by a tribe of Tatars known
   as the Tobas.
3. This emigration of northern intellectuals to
   South China greatly influenced the cultural
   progress of the Yangtze region.
4. Fà Xiàn was a Buddhist priest who traveled over-
   land to India and lived there for fourteen years.
5. Both Fà Xiàn and Xuān Zhuāng brought back many
   Buddhist classics, which they translated into
   Chinese.
6. Xuān Zhuāng went to India by land and returned
   by land, while Fà Xiàn went by land and returned
   by sea.

7. The Buddhism which came from India greatly influenced the sculpture of the Northern Wèi Kingdom.
8. At the time when Fà Xiǎn made his journey, many
   of the cities of Central Asia had become Buddhist, so he met many people who invited him to
   live in their homes.
9. Not only did many Chinese visit India during this
   period, but many Indians came to China, with the
   result that the Buddhist religion was established
   in China.
10. Just at the time that China was divided into a
    northern kingdom and a southern kingdom, the
    Roman Empire in the West was divided into east-
    ern and western empires.

Classroom Activities

1. Story Telling - Tell for a junior Chinese audi-
   ence some travel tale from western history sug-
   gested by the Chinese travelers to India during
   this period.
2. Map Talk - Using a wall map of Eurasia, give a
   brief talk on the relations between China and
   India in the 4th to 6th centuries A.D.

CHAPTER 13 - THE INFLUENCE OF BUDDHISM

Sentences for translation into Chinese

1. Canals served the double function of transportation and irrigation.
2. From the beginning of the fifth century to the
   end of the sixth century was a period of internal
   strife in China.
3. The diaries of these travellers contained much
   important information about the peoples and
   states of Central Asia.

4. If you visit Yúngǎng near Dàtóng in Shānxī, you can see the colossal Buddhas carved out of the face of the mountain.
5. Although South China was already acquainted with tea in the third century, it was not until the thirteenth century that the habit of tea drinking reached North China.
6. The sculptures of this period are far more natural than those of the Tang and Song periods.
7. While Fà Xiǎn was traveling in India, far away in Europe the half-civilized people known as Huns seized the city of Rome.
8. The Huns who seized Rome in 410 A.D. and the Xiōngnú who seized Zhāng Qiān in 138 B.C. belonged to the same tribe.

Classroom Activities

1. Debate - In the history of western civilization the ninth and tenth centuries are sometimes referred to as The Dark Ages. Some writers have applied the same term to the fifth and sixth centuries in China. Hold an informal debate on the appropriateness of this appelation.
2. Report - Look up the history of tea as given in the Encyclopedia Britannica or some similar source and make a report in Chinese to the class.
3. Report - Look up the history of early maps in various parts of the world and make a brief report to the class in Chinese.

CHAPTER 14 - THE SUI DYNASTY

Sentences for translation into Chinese

1. Although the period of the Six Dynasties was one of disorder, one cannot say that society made no progress.

2. Yáng Jiān, like Qín Shǐhuáng, regarded communica-
   tions as most important to national unity.
3. The rice of Húnán province could be brought by
   boat all the way from Chángshā to Chángān.
4. Before the invention of printing from wooden
   blocks, each book was laboriously copied by hand,
   and was very expensive.
5. Yáng Guāng not only had the books of the Zhōu
   and Hàn period copied, but also collected thou-
   sands of books written in recent times.
6. The amount of money spent by these two emperors
   on building their two capitals was very great.
7. When the burden of the people (the bitterness
   the people endure) becomes too great, they overthrow the dynasty.
8. When the population is small, administration of
   government is relatively simple, but as soon as
   the population becomes large, administration
   becomes complicated.
9. In the society of today, the three most crucial
   problems are still the same as in Súi times.
10. Until the transportation problem is solved,
    distribution of grain will remain a problem.

Classroom Exercises - Give a brief summary discussion
   on the following topics:

1. Zào yùnhé de zhòngyào (the importance of building
   the Canal)
2. Wénxúede jìnbù (advances in literature)
3. Súi cháode wàijiāo (foreign relations during the
   Súi dynasty)
4. Zhōngguo lìshǐshangde duǎnqī cháodài (short
   dynasties in Chinese history)
5. Jīngji wènti yǔ cháodài de yíngxiǎng (Economic
   problems and their influence on dynasties)
6. Bǐjiào Qín Súi, liǎngcháo, zài lìshǐshang de
   dìwei (compare the positions in history of the
   Ch'in and Sui dynasties)

CHAPTER 15 - THE TANG DYNASTY

Sentences for translation into Chinese

1. After the Jìn Dynasty, it was not until the Súi
   Dynasty that China was again united.
2. There are several similarities between the Hàn
   and the Táng Dynasties.
3. At the outset the Táng Dynasty had several capable rulers, but the last few emperors were
   incompetents.
4. The greatest weakness of many of China's rulers
   has been dependence on eunuchs and other unre-
   liable members of the imperial household.
5. China has had several very capable women rulers,
   but not one has had a good reputation in history.
6. Even the strongest dynasty has not lasted more
   than three or four hundred years.
7. When a strong dynasty like the Hàn or Táng falls,
   China always has a period of internal warfare
   and sometimes breaks up into a number of smaller
   states.
8. Because of his favorite concubine, Yáng Guìfēi,
   Táng Mínghuáng had to put down a rebellion and
   almost lost his throne.
9. When a Chinese dynasty became weak, the northern
   Tatars frequently seized the opportunity to set
   up a state in North China.
10. The Tatars were able to conquer North China
    because they had already been greatly influ-
    enced by Chinese culture.

Classroom Activities - Give brief summary discussions
of the following topics:

1. Nǚrén zai Zhōngguo húangcháoli de dìwei (the
   position of women in the Chinese imperial dynasty)
2. Yáng Gùi-fēi de gùshi (the story of Yang Gui-fei)
3. Ná Qín-Hàn, liǎngchái gen Súi-Táng, liǎngchái lái
   bǐjiào bǐjiào (compare the Qin-Han dynasties with
   the Sui-Tang dynasties)

4. Tuīfān Suí Chǎo, jiànlì Táng Chǎo de shìqing
   (the overthrow of the Sui and the founding of
   the Tang)
5. Táng Cháode mièwàng (the destruction of the Tang)

CHAPTER 16

THE FOREIGN RELATIONS OF THE TANG DYNASTY

Sentences for translation into Chinese

1. The Táng period is marked by territorial expansion in all directions. China incorporated
   Korea and South Manchuria on the north and part
   of Indo-China on the south. It also once again
   controlled the trade routes to the Northwest.
2. This was the period when Japan first came into
   contact with Chinese culture and began to borrow
   from it. Before the coming of the Chinese characters and the Confucian classics to Japan, she
   had no writing and no literature.
3. The Arabs learned many things from the Chinese,
   among them paper making and silk culture. They
   also learned mathematics and medicine from
   India. All these things they passed on to
   Europe.
4. During the seventh and eighth centuries Chinese
   civilization was at its height. China's power
   in Central Asia had reached the Caspian Sea.
   There was considerable intercourse between Táng
   China and other nations. At that time the Roman
   Empire had been broken into many small and
   powerless states. European civilization had
   degenerated. However, the Mohammedan Empire
   which arose in the seventh century was able to
   defeat the Chinese armies in Central Asia in
   751. After that, the Pamirs became the boundary
   between Táng power and Moslem power. We should
   note also that at approximately the same time,
   other Moslem armies were being defeated in

France. Consequently the Pyrenees Mountains became the boundary between Franks and Moslems in Europe.

Classroom Activities

1. Map Talk - The Imperial Domains of Han and Táng.
2. Report - Prepare a brief talk on the Pre-Táng Relations of China and Korea.
3. Report - Prepare a brief talk on the Pre-Táng Relations of China and Japan.
4. Report - Prepare a brief talk on Foreign Influences on Táng Culture.

Note: Sufficient material for these reports can be secured from such a work as Latourette: The Chinese, Their History and Culture, or Reischauer, Fairbank, East Asia: The Great Tradition, Volume One.

CHAPTER 18 - THE SONG DYNASTY

Note: Questions on the Text have so far been used to lead out the student and aid him in developing an ability to make clear and appropriate statements. Topics for Report and Discussion will provide for more extended expression. This elementary aid is now dropped as no longer necessary. Consequently more time and stress should be placed on the more advanced activity. Each report may well be discussed by the entire class in Chinese.

Sentences for translation into Chinese

1. The reforms which Wáng Ānshí attempted to put into effect were too advanced for those times. He proposed that the government should make an annual budget, so that it might know how much

taxes it would be necessary to collect. In
order to increase grain production, he had the
government loan money to framers to be repaid
after the harvest. He also had grain stored
away in granaries in years of good harvest. In
this way, there would be plenty to eat in years
of poor harvest.
2. There were several reasons why the Song Dynasty
   fell. One was that a large part of the government's income was spent on armament. A second
   reason was that the leaders who were opposed to
   Wang Anshi would not allow reforms to be carried
   out. Another was that able men refused to take
   responsibility for carrying on the government.
3. The Song Period is very famous for the porce-
   lains it produced. The porcelain process was
   invented in the Tang Dynasty, as was printing
   from carved wooden blocks. At the outset, the
   Confucian scholars opposed the printing of the
   Classics. It is strange that, although China
   invented moveable type in the Song Dynasty, the
   process was not used. Only after moveable type
   was brought from England early in the nineteenth century were books printed by this method.

Topics for Report and Discussion:

1. Qǐng nǐ shūoyishuo Sòng Cháode liǎngge shíqī
   (Please report on the two periods of the Song)
2. Qǐng shūo Wáng Ān-shíde gǎigé zhèngcè (Please
   report on the reforms of Wang An-shí)
3. Ná Wáng Mǎngde zhèngcè gēn Wáng Ān-shíde zhèngcè
   lái bǐjiào bǐjiào.
4. Qǐng shūo Běi Sòng shi zěmmayàng mǐewàngde
   (Please report on how the Northern Song was
   destroyed)
5. Běi Sòng shídài, Ōuzhōude qíngxing zěmmayàng
   (What was the situation in Europe during the
   Northern Song)

CHAPTER 19 - SOUTHERN SÒNG

Sentences for translation into Chinese

1. The story of Yùe Fēi and Qín Gùi shows how the
   struggle between two political parties can wreck
   the nation's foreign policy. Two separate states
   cannot last for long in China; the stronger of
   them will either drive out or assimilate the
   weaker within a few decades at most.
2. The location of China's capital has a close relation to her national policy. If she considers
   Manchuria a part of China proper and feels able
   to hold onto it then she will locate her capital
   in a northern city such as Peking. If she is
   interested only in holding onto what is known
   as "the Eighteen Provinces", then she may establish her capital in the Yangtse Valley.
3. Commercial relations with the surrounding nations
   increased. During the Táng Dynasty many foreign
   merchants from distant lands had come to China's
   ports. Chinese ships, however, usually kept
   close to the Chinese Coast. In the Sòng Period
   the continental routes to the west were cut off,
   so Chinese merchants increasingly used the
   southern water routes to go to Malaya, India
   and even Arabia.

Topics for Report and Discussion - Make brief reports
   on the following topics and discuss each in Chinese
   after classroom presentation:

1. Zhōngguode zāihuāng wèntí (the problem of natural
   calamities in China)
2. Zhōngguode tiánzhì wèntí (the question of land
   systems)
3. Shíliáng fēnpèi wèntí (the question of food
   distribution)
4. Shuǐlì wèntí (the question of taxes)
5. Jūnzhì wèntí (the question of military system)

6. Yuè Fēi de gùshi (the story of Yue Fei)
7. Nán Sòng de mièwàng (the fall of Southern Song)
8. Nán Sòng wénhùa chéngji (the level of culture in the Southern Song)
9. Nán Sòngde gōngshāngyè (business and labor in the Southern Song)

Special Report - Prepare an outline (in either Chinese or English) of the cultural, not political, development of China through the Sòng period. Give a talk from this outline.

CHAPTERS 20 & 21 - THE YUÁN DYNASTY

Sentences for translation into Chinese

1. In the 13th century the greater part of Asia and Europe were conquered by the Mongols. These Mongols were descendants of the Xiūngnú, and the Turki who had raided China during the Hàn and Táng periods.
2. Kubilai Khan even attempted to invade Japan. Of course he had to rely on the Chinese people to build his ships and be his sailors, for Mongols have neither knowledge nor the experience in navigation. His two expeditions both met with overwhelming defeat.
3. Kubilai had great respect for Chinese culture and sought the aid of Chinese scholars, but most of them scorned serving a half-civilized Mongol. Nevertheless, during the Yuán Dynasty two types of literature were developed in China which had not been highly regarded before: drama and fiction. These arose from the common people, not from the literati, and even the uncultured Mongols could appreciate them.

Topics for report and discussion - Make a brief
  report on the following topics and follow each
  report with classroom discussion in Chinese:

1. Chéngjìsì Hànde shēngpíng hé gōngzùo (The life
   and works of Jenghis Khan)
2. Zhōngguo wénhùa yǔ Méngǔrén de yíngxiang (the
   influence of Chinese culture on the Mongolians)
3. Wèishemma Yúan Cháode lìshǐ nèmma dǔan - méiyǒu
   yìbǎinían jìu meiwangle? (Explain the brevity of
   the Yuan dynasty--it fell after only less than
   100 years)
4. Qǐng shūo Yúan Cháo hǎijūn qīnlùe Rìběn de
   yùanzhēng (Explain the invasion of Japan by the
   Yuan navy)
5. Look up the story of Marco Polo, learn the major
   facts, and retell it in simple Chinese.

Special project - following is the story of a famous
  Chinese traveler of the Mongol Period. Since it
  involves certain new terms, a vocabulary is append-
  ed. The story may be translated into Chinese as it
  stands as an exercise in translation, or it may be
  used as background material for telling the story
  in one's own words in Chinese. This project may
  be spread over the two chapter assignments dealing
  with the Mongol Period (Chapters 20-21).

LONG SPRING

  Jenghis Khan, founder of the Yuan Dynasty, left
off his conquest of China and withdrew his armies
because of troubles in the west. There is a very
interesting story connected with his western cam-
paign which I am going to tell you.
  At that time in the province of Shantung there
was a Taoist priest more than seventy years of age
by the name of Ch'iu Ch'u-chi. People called him
"Long Spring". This old priest was famous for his
great piety. Emperors of both Kin and Sung Dynasties

had invited him to come and expound the Taoist doc-
trines to them, but he wouldn't go. In 1217 Jenghis
Khan sent a messenger from the Mongol capital of
Karakorum to China to invite him. He accepted the
invitation and immediately set out with 18 acolytes.
He arrived at Yenching, the present Peking, in mid-
winter. He was told that it was very cold in Mongolia and urged to delay in Peking until it got
warmer before going on. He stayed in Peking for a
couple of months, but as soon as the weather warmed
up started on again.

He hadn't gone far beyond the Great Wall when a
messenger arrived from Kuyuk, the younger brother of
Jenghis, saying that the Great Khan had already gone
to the Naiman country, and asking the priest to follow him there. At the same time Kuyuk invited him
to come first to Eastern Mongolia as he also would
like to see him. Ch'iu Ch'ang-ch'un went, stayed a
few days, and then continued his journey westward.
The original trip from Peking to Karakorum was less
than a thousand miles, but the trip he must now under-
take was nearly 3000 miles. This road was through
high mountains and across the desert and very rough.
Sometimes he rode in a cart, sometimes on horseback,
sometimes in a mule-litter, and sometimes on foot.

As he traveled along, winter came on again; but
this time not even winter could stop him. Although
he was an old man, his spirit was still strong. He
crossed mountains and forded torrents, he traveled
under the moon and stars; difficulties and hardships
held no fear for him. He forged ahead over the
14,000 foot Altai range, through snowstorms and
bitter winds.

It took him over a year to make the journey but
he finally caught up with Jenghis in the vicinity
of the Oxus River, where he stayed for several months
conversing frequently with the Great Khan.

It is said that once Jenghis Khan asked his
advice on how to rule the world. He said, "The only
way to rule the world is to love men." Jenghis

listened, thought it over, and remarked, "Quite right.
Only love can win the hearts of men. I must write
your words down and not forget them." Unfortunately
the Khan was so busy killing men that he didn't find
time to love them.

Later Ch'iu Ch'ang-ch'un returned to Yenching.
Yuan T'aitsu appointed him head of the entire Taoist
sect, had him live in a temple at Yenching, the name
of which was The Long Spring Temple. It is now
known as the White Cloud Temple. There the old
priest died at the age of eighty; and strangely
enough, Jenghis Khan died in the same year.

If you should go to Peking, you must certainly
visit the White Cloud Temple. It is still the
largest Taoist temple in Peking, and contains an
image of Ch'iu Ch'ang-ch'un. At New Year time there
is much going on. The 19th of the first moon of the
lunar calendar is Ch'iu Ch'ang-ch'un's birthday.
There is a swarm of visitors. In the temple is a
building, on three sides of which are hung lanterns
depicting the story of Ch'iu Ch'ang-ch'un's visit
ot Jenghis Khan. It's most interesting.

Supplementary Vocabulary

leave off, cease . . . . . fàngqì
Taoist priest . . . . . . dàoshī
piety, virtue . . . . . . dàode
currently, at the time . . dāngshí
accept (an invitation) . . dáyìng
accolyte . . . . túdi
set out, leave for . . . . chūfā
mule-litter . . . . lúotúojiào
age (of life) . . . . . . suìshu
climb mountains . . . . . dēng shān
ford rivers . . . . shèshǔi
hardship . . . . láokǔ
rule the world . . . . . zhìlǐ tīanxià
only, sole . . . . wéiyīde
win, gain . . . . dédào

be busy about, be con-
  stantly thinking about . . . gùde
at New Year's time . . . . . . guóniánde shíhou
lunar calendar . . . . yīnlì

Proper Names

Kuyuk . . . . Guìyóu
Naiman . . . . Nàimàn
Altai Mountains . . . . . . Aĕrtái Shān
Oxus River . . . . Amù hé
White Cloud Temple . . . . . Báiyùn guān

CHAPTER 22 - THE MING DYNASTY

Sentences for translation into Chinese

1. The policy of the Mongol rulers of China included these two principles:
   a. Although they themselves were unable to take
      on Chinese culture to any great extent, they
      nonetheless respected it and sought the aid
      of Chinese scholars in establishing their
      rule.
   b. They divided the people into four classes,
      giving better treatment to those groups
      which had aided in the conquest of the Sung
      Empire and the worst treatment to the people
      of Southern Sung who had so long opposed them.
2. The rebellion which established the Ming Dynasty
   sprang from the common people not from the upper
   classes. It was led by a former Buddhist priest
   by the name of Zhū Yuán-zhāng. Although he was
   very able as a military leader and as an admin-
   istrator, he lived all his days in fear of being
   dethroned.
3. The most illustrious ruler of the Ming Dynasty
   was not its founder but his fourth son Chéng zŭ,
   whose reign title was Yŏnglò. He dethroned his

nephew Huìdì because the latter attempted to
abolish the power of the royal princes, each of
whom ruled a section of the country. Chéng zǔ
defeated the Mongols and reestablished Chinese
suzerainty over Annam.

Topics for outside reading (in English) and report in
    Chinese:

1. Měngǔrén zěmmayàng duìdài Zhōngguo rén? (How the
   Mongols treated the Chinese)
2. Míngchūde zhèngzhì zhìdu (the political system
   of the early Ming)
3. Míng Chéngzǔde gōngzuo (the accomplishments of
   Ming Chengzu)
4. Ná Míng Cháo qiāndū de shìqing gēn yǐqian cháodài
   qiāndū lai bǐjiao bǐjiao. (Compare the Ming shift
   of the capital with earlier dynasties movement
   of the capital)
5. Yúan Cháode fǔbài (the corruption of the Yuan
   dynasty)
6. Míng Cháo huángdìde ròdǐan (the weaknesses of
   the emperors of the Ming)
7. Ná Míng Cháode lǐngtǔ gēn Táng Cháode lǐngtǔ lai
   bǐjiao bǐjiao (Compare the territory of the Ming
   with the Tang)
8. Zhōngguo lìshǐshang yǒu píngmín qilai zuò tiānzǐ
   de rén (Report on those persons in Chinese history
   who rose from common status to being the Son of
   Heaven)

CHAPTER 23

FOREIGN RELATIONS DURING THE MING

Translate into Chinese

China has usually been more interested in the land
than in the sea. On the continent her armies went

as far as the Caspian Sea on the west, Korea on the
east and Indochina on the south. During the Ming
Dynasty however she showed an interest in sailing
the South Seas. A palace eunuch by the name of Zhèng
Hé was sent out to visit the countries of southeast
Asia and persuade them to accept the suzerainty of
China. Over a period of thirty years he made seven
expeditions, visiting many counties in the South
Seas, and even going as far as Ceylon, Arabia, and
the east coast of Africa.

These expeditions were similar to those of the
English Admiral Sir Francis Drake a century and a
half later to the coasts of North and South America.
If a state accepted China's overlordship and paid
tribute, it was treated as an ally. If it did not,
it was forced into submission. Zhèng Hé, on his
third expedition, seized the king of Ceylon and took
him back to Nanking. He also brought back much
information about the sea routes, harbors and conditions of navigation. In addition, like Zhāng Qiān
and Fà Xiǎn, he reported to the emperor on the peoples of foreign countries, their customs and products.

Suddenly about 1430, these expeditions ceased, for
what reason is not known, possibly because they
cost a great deal of money or because other officials
were jealous of Zhèng Hé's fame. From that time on,
China had little intercourse with western nations
until they in their turn forced her to open her
ports to them in the first half of the nineteenth
century.

Topics for outside reading (in English) and report
  in Chinese:

  1. Míng Cháo yǔ Rìběn de guānxi (Relations between
     the Ming Dynasty and Japan)
  2. Zhèng Hé xìa xīyáng (Cheng Ho Journeys to the
     West)

3. Xīyángde Xuézhě láidao Zhōngguo (Western scholars arrive in China)
4. Míng Cháode de mièwàng (the fall of the Ming)
5. Xīyángde shānglǚ chūcì láidao Zhōngguode hǎikǒu (Western traders come to a Chinese port for the first time)

CHAPTER 24 - THE THOUGHT OF THE MING DYNASTY

Translate into Chinese:

THE STORY OF THE LOST TRIBE

When Li Zì-chéng rebelled and led his army against Peking, the emperor Chóngzhēn sent appeals for help all over the country. One of the forces sent to save the dynasty was a small group of three hundred men from Shānxī province. They marched through the mountains and came out on the plain west of Peking just in time to learn that the Manchus had taken the city and the emperor had committed suicide on the Coal Hill.

The three hundred men, attempting to return home through the mountains, were prevented by Manchu forces sent to take them. However, they hid in a small valley, and the Manchu soldiers passed them by on the north and on the south and failed to discover them. Since their number was so small, the Manchus soon abandoned the search and forgot about them. After some years, when the Manchus had conquered the entire country and were no longer afraid of rebellions, word was brought that this band was still living in a valley known as "Three Slopes". The Ching Dynasty punished them by decreeing that they should live in that one valley forever and should have no contact with the outer world. Their wives and families were brought to live there with them. They were allowed to govern themselves, but

once a year the headman went out to a nearby district
capital to pay taxes for the whole tribe.

In 1912 they were liberated by the Chinese Revolution.
They were then still wearing the style of clothing
common during the Ming Dynasty, and the women of the
tribe did their hair as the Ming women did theirs,
a style no longer used in China today but very much
resembling that used by Japanese women. Even their
speech differed from that of the surrounding villages.
We might say that a group of Ming Dynasty people had
been buried among the hills for 250 years and then
suddenly brought back to life.

One is reminded of the American story of Rip Van
Winkle who went to sleep in the mountains during the
time when America was still a group of British
colonies, and woke up several decades later after
the American Revolution had taken place. I imagine
the "Lost Tribe" found it about as hard to fit into
modern Chinese society as Rip Van Winkle did to
adapt himself to the changes in 18th century America.

Topics for outside reading (in English) and report
in Chinese:
1. Wáng Yángmíngde sīxiǎng (the thought of Wang
   Yang-ming)
2. Míng cháode měishù (the fine arts of the Ming)
3. Míng cháode wénxuéjiā (the writers of the Ming)
4. Běijīngde lìshǐ- cóng Zhōu cháo dào xiànzài
   (the history of Peking from the Chou to the
   present) See Juliet Bredon's PEKING.

CHAPTER 25 - THE QÍNG DYNASTY

Translate into Chinese

THE RISE OF THE MANCHUS

The founder of the Manchu state was Nurhachi, a
brave soldier, able leader, and brilliant organizer.
By 1616 he had conquered most of Manchuria and
driven the Chinese south of the Great Wall. In
1625 he established his capital at Mukden and gave
his dynasty the name Golden to indicate that it was
to continue the Jīn Dynasty of the Jurchen Tatars
from whom he claimed to be descended. This title
he later changed to Clear. Since the Chinese
dynasty was named Brilliant, this meant that he considered himself of equal rank. It was done also to
avoid offending the Mongols who had not forgotten
that the Jīn Dynasty had prevented Genghis Khan from
conquering Manchuria.

Nurhachi greatly respected Chinese civilization and
tried in every way to learn from it and to copy its
organization. Just as the Japanese in the 8th and
9th centuries had copied the Táng culture even to
building a new capital modelled after the Chinese
capital at Xīan, so the Manchus in the 17th century
immitated Chinese culture and built their new capital of Mukden (Shěnyáng) on the pattern of Peking.

The Manchus did not attempt to conquer China Proper
until the country was weakened by revolts. In 1644
Peking was seized by a rebel army led by Lǐ Zì-chéng.
The Míng general defending the Great Wall, Wú Sān-gūi,
invited the Manchus to come to the help of the Míng
emperor. The allied forces drove the rebels out of
Peking, but once the Manchus were inside China they
refused to retire to their own country. Instead
they put the two-year old grandson of Nurhachi on
the throne of China as the Emperor Shùnzhì. After
that it took them about forty years to conquer the
whole of China.

Topics for outside reading (in English) and report
  in Chinese:
  1. Mǎnzúde láiyúan (the origin of the Manchus)
  2. Mǎnzhōu yǔ Cháoxiān de jiāojì (relations between
     Manchuria and Korea)
  3. Nǔérhāchī jiànlì Jīnguó (Nurhachi establishes
     the Jīn State)
  4. Lǐ Zìchéng zàofǎn (the rebellion of Li Zicheng)
  5. Qīng Cháo chūqīde zhèngzhì (the politics of the
     Early Qīng)
  6. Kāng Xī huángdì de gōngzùo (the accomplishments
     of the Kang Xi emperor)

CHAPTER 26

RELATIONS BETWEEN THE QĪNG DYNASTY AND THE WEST

Translate into Chinese

Someone asked a Chinese student and an American
student what were the basic causes of the unhappy
relations between China and the western nations in
the first half of the nineteenth century. The
Chinese student said that the real reason was the
commercial greed and national pride of occidentals.
The American student said that it lay in the

arrogance, ignorance and corruption of Chinese officials. Both answers have an element of truth in
them but neither is an adequate explanation of the
situation.

We must consider conditions in China and in the
west at that time.

1. A century earlier the Chīng Empire was the most
   powerful state in the whole world. By the middle
   of the 19th century it had so degenerated that it
   was almost overthrown by a rebellion from within
   and was constantly being defeated by a handful
   of European soldiers.

2. A century earlier Chinese culture was equal to
   or superior to any culture in the world. Living
   conditions were better than in the west. But
   during the century previous to 1850, the occident
   had experienced the so-called Industrial Revolution. There resulted a remarkable improvement in
   standard of living.

3. From an economic point of view, China had prac-
   tically everything she needed within her own
   borders. But the Industrial Revolution had
   greatly increased the needs of Europe which could
   only be supplied by overseas trade. So while
   commercial relations were undesirable to China,
   they were an absolute necessity to Europe.

4. The geographical discoveries in the 15th, 16th
   and 17th centuries had made occidentals realize
   that they lived in a much larger world than their
   ancestors. China's horizon, on the other hand,
   was very little wider than it had been in Han
   times.

5. China had never before dealt with any foreign
   nation as an equal. The relationship had always

been that of overlord and tributary. There was
no such thing as international law in the modern
sense. The occidental states however had been
developing a set of customs to govern the relations between equal states.

In view of these facts we cannot say that the unfor-
tunate relations were the fault of one side or the
other. They were due to the failure of both sides
to understand the very different background and
viewpoint of the other side.

Topics for outside reading (in English) and report
   in Chinese:
   1. Suǒwèi Yāpiàn Zhànzhēng (the so-called Opium War)
   2. Zhōng-wài sīxiǎng chōngtú (the conflicts between
      Chinese and foreign thought)
   3. Ná Xīyángde dìguozhǔyì gēn Zhōngguode dìguozhǔyì
      lái bǐjiao bǐjiao (Compare Western and Chinese
      imperialism)
   4. Nánjīng Tiáoyūe (the Treaty of Nanking)
   5. Jìn-yān wèntí (the problem of the prohibition
      of opium)
   6. Lǐnshi-cáipàn-quán (Extraterritoriality)
   7. Dìshíjǐu shìjì qiánbànqī Měiguo yǔ Zhōngguo de
      jiaojì (relations between America and China in
      the first half of the 19th century)

               CHAPTER 27 - THE RESULTS OF DIPLOMACY

Translate into Chinese

                    THE TAIPING REBELLION

As we have noticed, the decline of the Chīng Dynasty
led to internal disorders. The greatest of these
was the Tàipíng Rebellion which lasted from 1848 to
1865. It's leader had listened to the teachings of
Christian missionaries. Under the influence of these

religious ideas, he planned to drive out the Manchus
and establish a democratic society in China. Some
of his ideas however were rather extreme. For instance, he worshipped God as the Heavenly Father,
called Jesus the Son of Heaven, and regarded himself
as the Younger Brother of Jesus.

This rebellion was also a revolt of the common
people against the landlords, merchants and gentry.
It was probably the promises of social and economic
reform which influenced the masses most strongly
and made them support this movement. If Hóng Xiù-
quán had shown a genius for organization and political leadership, he might have succeeded in over-
throwing the Manchu government. In the end, however, all conservative elements united to oppose him.
Many of the common people also had suffered great
losses in the course of the rebellion, so they began
to turn against him too. Moreover the foreign
powers feared that an overthrow of the Manchu Dynasty would upset their special privileges obtained by
means of treaties, so they supported the Chīng
Dynasty.

Many able Chinese leaders gave their support to the
Manchus because they feared the extreme views of
the Taipings. A new army, organized and drilled by
foreign officers and led by Chinese generals finally
defeated the Taiping army. The rebellion had lasted
nearly seventeen years, layed waste great areas of
south and central China, and cost the lives of
twenty million Chinese.

Today the Chinese People's Republic believes that
it has completed the revolution which Húng Syòuchywán
started a century ago.

Topics for outside reading (in English) and report
in Chinese:

1. Tàipíng Tīanguó yùndòng yǔ xiàndàide
   Gòngchǎnzhǔyì (The Heavenly Kingdom of the
   Taipings and its connection with present-day
   Communism)
2. Tīanjīn hé Běijīng tíaoyūe (the Tiantsin and
   Peking Treaties)
3. Rùkǒushui wèntí (the problem of tariffs)
4. Jīdūjìao yǔ Zhōngguo zhǎnkāi de gūanxi (the
   relationship between Christianity and the
   opening up of China)
5. Sǔowèi bùpíngděng tíaoyūe yǔ bùpíngděnge
   wàijīao tánpàn de gūanxi (the connection between
   the so-called Unequal Treaties and unequal
   diplomatic negotiations)
6. Yǎpiàn wèntí (the problem of opium)

CHAPTER 28 - THE LAST YEARS OF THE QĪNG

Translate into Chinese

TIMES HAVE CHANGED

When European and American merchants first tried to
trade with China, they came into contact with a nation which had never before recognized any other
nation as its equal. There was much justification
for the condescending attitude of the Ching rulers
toward outsiders. China's immediate neighbors were
all smaller and weaker nations which had derived
much of their culture from China. Most of them
had at times been tributary to China. They looked
up to China as a powerful and generally beneficent
overlord whom they had little desire to challenge.

The occidental, however, came from an area in which
political, economic and cultural leadership had

passed from hand to hand through the centuries, and
no one nation held a monopoly on it. The Roman Empire had passed away and the leadership of the
European community fell to the Germanic peoples.
The <u>Italian</u> <u>States</u> led culturally for a long period;
then Spain through her geographical discoveries
built a huge overseas commercial and political empire. Spain's leadership was challenged by the Dutch
and then snatched away by the English. So when the
merchants came to China, whether they were Spaniards,
Portuguese, Hollanders, Englishmen or Frenchmen,
they were arrogant, demanding and displayed a strong
tendency to exploit other peoples for their own
advantage with little regard for the interests of
the other party.

In such a situation, what could be expected to result other than the frictions and jealousies, the
fears and hatreds, the diplomatic intrigues and open
warfare which actually did mark the first century of
relations between China and the West?

The remarkable fact is that China came out of the
ordeal intact, that within the century she gained
back most of the rights she had signed away, that
today she is one of the world's great powers.
Clearly this is due in part to circumstances beyond
China's power of determination. It is due in considerable degree to the fact that Russia, once an
eager participant in dismembering China, found it
in accord with her national and ideological interest to build China up as the dominant power in the
Far East. Nevertheless, the fact must be faced,
that the China which was a few decades ago the "Sick
Man of Asia" now poses as great a challenge to the
world community of nations as a century ago did
Húng Syòuchywán and his Tàipíng Tyāngwó to the
Manchu regime in China.

Supplementary Vocabulary

any	rènhé
proud	jīaoào
at last, after all. . . .	jīujìng
benevolent	réndé
leadership	lǐngdǎoquán
Germanic peoples	Rìèrmàn rén
supremacy, tyranny . . .	bàquán
violate, encroach	qīnfàn
exploit, fleece	bōxiāo
conspiracy, intrigue . .	yīnmóu

Topics for outside reading (in English) and report in Chinese:

1. Jìndài Rìbénde xīngqǐ (the rise of modern Japan)
2. Yìhétúan yùndòng (The Boxer movement)
3. Zhōng-Rì Cháoxīan de chōngtú (conflict between China and Japan over Korea)
4. Qīng Cháo yǔ Èguo de jīaojì (relations between the Ching dynasty and Russia)
5. Qīngmòde Wéixīn Yùndòng (the Modernization Movement in Late Qing)
6. Xī Tàihòu (the Empress Dowager)
7. Lǐ Hóngzhāng (Li Hong-chang)
8. Kāng Yǒuwéi (K'ang Yu-wei)
9. Sūn Wén/Sūn Zhōngshān (Sun Yat-sen)
10. Qīng Cháo zài Zhōngguo lìshǐshang de dìwei (the position of the Ching dynasty in Chinese history)

ài-bào

A

ài	爱	V:	to love, like
àiguó	～国	VO:	to be patriotic
àixīn	～心	N:	love, tender regard

àn	岸	N:	shore, bank
héan	河～	N:	river bank
hǎian	海～	N:	seashore

àn	暗	SV:	to be dark
ànzhe	～着	A:	secretly

B

bá	拔	V:	to pluck, pull out
báchulai	～出来	RV:	to pluck out
báxialai	～下来	RV:	to tear down

báihuà	白话	N:	vernacular, non-literary
báihuàwén	～～文	N:	vernacular literature

báirì	白日	TW:	daytime

bǎixìng	百姓	N:	common people
láobǎixìng	老～～	N:	common people

bàn	半	M:	half
bàndǎo	～岛	N:	peninsula
bàndàorshang		PW:	half-way, in the midst of
bànkāihua	～开化	SV:	to be half-civilized

bāokuò	包括	V:	to include

bǎo	保	V:	to protect, guarantee
bǎohu	～护	V:	to protect
báojǔ		V:	to recommend, guarantee
báoshǒu		V/SV:	to protect, preserve; conservative
bǎocún	保存	V:	to preserve, maintain

bǎo	宝	SV:	precious
bǎobèi	～贝	SV/N:	to be precious, precious one
bǎoguì	～贵	SV:	to be precious, valuable

bào	报	V/N:	to report; newspaper
bàogào	～告	V/N:	to report; report
bàozhǐ	～纸	N:	newspaper

bào	抱	V:	to carry (in one's arms)

běijìn	北进	V:	to drive northward (mil.)
bèi	辈	M:	generation
bèijǐng	背景	N:	background
bèiwo	被窝	N:	quilt
běn	本	•N:	root, own, origin
běnbù		N:	basic area
běnjiā	～家	N:	own home, family
běnguó	～国	N:	native land, own country
běnrén	～人	N:	oneself
běnwén	～文	N:	the original language
běndì	～地	N:	this region here
běnlǐng	～领	N:	native ability
běnshi	～事	N:	ability
běnxìng	～性	N:	natural disposition, nature
běnqián	～钱	N:	capital
běnlái	～来	MA:	originally
bǐcǐ (bǐ)	彼此	A:	mutually, one with another
bǐ	比	CV:	compared with
bǐdeshàng		RV:	to be comparable, can be compared with
bǐbushàng		RV:	to be incomparable
bǐjiào	比较	V/N:	to compare; comparison
bìzhì	币制	N:	monetary system
biàn	变	V:	to change
biànchéng	～成	V:	to change into, become
biànfǎ	～法	VO:	to reform (lit: change law)
biànhua	～化	V/N:	to change, reform; changes
(see gǎibiàn)			
biànli	便利	SV:	to be convenient
biǎo	表	V:	to manifest, express
biǎo	表	N:	clock, watch, chart
biǎochū		RV:	to show forth
biǎomíng	表明	V:	to state clearly
biǎoshì	～示	V:	to express, show
bié	别	•N:	other
biéchu	～处	N:	elsewhere
biéren	～人	N:	other person
biéde	～的	N:	other, else

bīng	兵	N:	soldier
bīngqì	～器	N:	weapon
bīngchuán	～船	N:	naval vessel

| bóshi | 博士 | N: | doctor of philosophy, Ph.D. |

bù	不	A:	not
budébu	～得～	V:	cannot do otherwise than
búguò	～过	MA:	merely
búduànde	～断地	A:	unceasingly
buzhībujuéde		MA:	unwittingly, unconsciously
burán	～然	V:	it is not so, oh no.
(yào)burán		MA:	otherwise
búxìng	～幸	SV:	to be unfortunate, unlucky
butóng	～同	SV:	to be unlike, dissimilar
búwài	～外	MA:	exclusively, nothing but

bù	部	M:	section, class, of books
bùfen	～分	M/N:	portion, section, part
quánbù	全～	N:	the entire lot

C

| cáizhèng | 财政 | N: | finance |

| cāngfáng | 仓房 | N: | granary |

| cáng | 藏 | V: | to hide |

cǎo	草	N:	grass, straw
cǎo xié	～鞋	N:	straw shoe
cǎo rén	～人	N:	straw man

| céng | 曾 | A: | once, at some previous time |

| cèliàng | 测量 | V/N: | to survey, surveying |

chǎn	产	V:	to produce
chǎnyè	～业	N:	property, possessions
chūchǎn	出～	N:	product, produce

| chánzú | 缠足 | VO: | bind feet |

chángzhǎng(chǎng)	厂长	N:	foreman, manager (factory)
chángjiǔ	长久	A:	for a long time
hǎojiǔ	好久	MA:	for a long time

| chāo | 抄 | V: | to copy |
| chāoxiě | ～写 | V: | to copy(by writing) |

cháo	朝	°N:	dynasty
cháodài	～代	N:	dynasty
chē	车	N:	cart, vehicle
chēzi	～子	N:	cart (diminutive)
chè	撤	V:	to withdraw, draw back
chèbīng	～兵	VO:	to withdraw troops
chèjìn	～进	RV:	to withdraw within (limits)
chén	沉	V:	to sink
chénmò	～没	V:	to sink (a ship)
dǎchénle	打～了	RV:	sank (a ship)
chènzhe jīhui		CV-O:	avail oneself of opportunity
chēng	称	V:	to call, address (a person) be called
chēngwéi	～为	V:	to call, be called
chéng	城	N:	city, walled city, city wall
chénglóu	～楼	N:	city gate tower
chéngshì	～市	N:	city, metropolis
chéngxià	～下	PW:	in front of/outside of city
chéngqiáng	～墙	N:	city wall
chéng	成	V:	to become, establish
chénglì	～立	V:	to establish
chéngguó	～国	VO:	to establish dynasty/state
chéngdu	程度	N:	grade, level, degree
chéngwei yìtǐ		VO:	to become one body
biàn...chéng...		V:	to transform...into...
chéngrèn	承认	V:	to acknowledge, recognize
chéngyì	诚意	SV:	to be sincere
chīshi	吃食	N:	food, eatables
chōngtu	冲突	N:	obstacle, clash
chóngbài	崇拜	V:	to worship
chóuzi	绸子	N:	silk goods
chóukuǎn	筹款	VO:	raise funds
chū	初	°N:	beginning
chūqī	～期	TW:	beginning of period, earlier period
Qīngchū	清～	TW:	beginning of Qing dynasty
chūxué	～学	V:	to start studying

chū	出	V:	to emerge, produce, manifest
chūyáng	～洋	VO:	cross the ocean, go abroad
chūmíng		VO/SV:	to be famous
chūchǎn	～产	N:	products
chūshǐ	～使	V:	to be sent on a mission
chūshēn	～身	VO:	to enter public service
chūqí	～奇	SV:	to be marvelous, strange
chuán	传	V:	to transmit, hand down
chuándá	～达	V:	to carry a message
chuánxiaqu	～下去	RV:	to pass on (down)
chuánguoqu	～过去	RV:	to get (an idea) over
chuánjiào	～教	VO:	to propagate religion
chuándào	～道	VO:	to preach
xuānchuán	宣～	V:	to propagate
chuánjiaoshī		N:	missionary
chuángqián	床前	N:	in frint of the bed
chuǎng(or chuáng)		V:	to create, initiate
chuǎngbàn	创办	V:	to initiate, create
chuǎnglì	创立	V:	to establish, found
cí	词	N:	poem (different from shī)
cí	瓷磁	N:	porcelain; magnetism
cíqì	瓷器	N:	porcelainware
cíqijiàng	～～匠	N:	porcelain maker
cízhēn	磁针	N:	mariner's compass
cíai	慈爱	N:	love, mercy
cìjī	刺激	N:	stimulus
cūn	村	°N:	village
cūnzi	～子	N:	village
cūnzhuāng	～庄	N:	village
cún	存	V:	to store up
cúnqilai	～起来	RV:	to store up
cúnzài	～在	V:	to be extant, be preserved
cúnzai	～在	V:	to store in

<u>D</u>

dāying	答应	V:	to reply, assent
dá	达	°V:	to succeed, attain
dádao mùdi		VO:	to succeed in one's purpose
dácheng mùdi		VO:	to attain one's purpose

dǎ	打	V:	to strike, fight
dǎbài	～败	RV:	to defeat, be defeated
dǎchénle	～沉了	RV:	to sink (ship) in battle
dǎdǎo	～倒	RV:	to overthrow
dǎdào	～到	RV:	to fight (all the way) to
dǎfa	～发	V:	to send, dispatch
dǎfúle	～服了	RV:	to conquer
dǎjìn	～进	RV:	to fight one's way into
dǎjià	～架	V:	to quarrel
dǎléi	～雷	VO:	to thunder
dǎliè	～猎	VO:	to go hunting
dǎpíngle	～平了	RV:	"pacified", subdued
dáqilai	～起来	RV:	to start fighting
dǎ qízi	～旗子	VO:	to unfurl flag, fly a flag
dǎjī	～击	V:	to shock, strike
dǎxialai	～下来	RV:	to succeed in conquering
dǎyú	～鱼	VO:	to catch fish
dà	大	SV:	to be large
dàdā-xiáoxiǎo(de)		N:	big ones and little ones
dàduōshu	大多数	N:	the vast majority
dàchén	大臣	N:	high official
dàlù	～陆	N:	continent
dàmǐ	～米	N:	rice
dàqilai	～起来	RV:	to grow great, increase
dàyuē	～约	A:	probably
dài	代	M:	period, dynasty
cháodài	朝～	N:	dynasty
niándài	年～	N:	period of years, duration
jìndài	近～	TW:	recent times
gǔdài	古～	TW:	ancient times
shídài	时～	N:	period, era
xiàndài	现～	TW:	present time
dāng	当	V:	ought, to act as, in, at
dāng bīng	～兵	VO:	to become a soldier, join the army
dāng héshang		VO:	to become a Buddhist priest
dāngchū	～初	MA:	at the outset
dāngzuò	～作	V:	to treat as
dǎngzhu	挡住	V:	to block, bar
dǎng	党	M:	political party
dǎngpài	～派	N:	political party

dǎng (cont.)

  Guómíndǎng   N: National People's Party (KMT)
  Gòngchándǎng   N: Communist Party

dāo   刀   N: sword
  dāo   M: blow, stroke
  dāozi   ＜子 N: knife

dǎo   岛   N: island
  háidǎo (hǎi)   N: island
  bàndǎo   半＜ N: peninsula

dǎoluàn   搗乱 V: to cause disturbance

dàoliǎo(r) 到了 A: finally, in the end

dé   得   V: to get, obtain, attain
  dédào   ＜到 RV: to obtain, gain
  déshèng ＜胜 VO: to obtain a victory
  dézhao   ＜着 RV: to obtain, get

děng   等   N: marks the conclusion of list
  děngdeng ＜＜ N: etc.

dí   敌   °N: enemy
  díren   ＜人 N: enemy
  díguó   ＜国 N: enemy country
  díshǒu   ＜手 N: rival, equal

dǐkàng   抵抗 V: to oppose, resist

dì   地   N: earth, land
  dìbu   ＜步 N: condition, point
  dìdòng   ＜洞 N: pit (in the ground)
  dìfang guān   N: local official
  dìlǐ   ＜理 N: geography
  dìlǐxué ＜理学 N: geography
  dìpán   ＜盘 N: (extent of) territory
  dìtú   ＜图 N: map
  dìwei   ＜位 N: position, rank
  dìzhǔ   ＜主 N: landlord

dìxiōng   弟兄 N: brothers, brethren

diànxiàn 电线 N: telegraph wires

diāokē (diāokè) V/N: to sculpt, carve; sculpture

diàoxia   掉下 RV: to fall off, drop off

dīngzi	钉子	N:	nail, snag
dìng	定	V:	to settle, decide
dìnglì	订立	V:	to establish, decide upon, draw up
dìnglì tiáoyuē		VO:	to sign a treaty
dìngwéi	定为	V:	to decide upon ... as
dìngzuì	～罪	VO:	to judge culpability
dōnglái	东来	V:	to move eastward
dǒng(de)	懂	V:	to understand
dòngwù	动	N:	moving things, animals
dú	毒	SV:	to be poisonous, evil
dúyào	～药	N:	poison
dúlì	独立	V:	to become independent
dúshū	读书	VO:	read books, read
dǔqián	赌钱	VO:	to gamble
duìhuàn	对换	V:	to exchange, barter
duōqilai	多起来	V:	to grow more numerous
duǒbì	躲避	V:	to avoid (mén)
duǒkāi	～开	V:	to get out of way, withdraw

E

| erqiě | 而且 | A: | also, moreover |

F

fā	发	V:	to give out, distribute
fābīng	～兵	VO:	to send a military force
fādá	～达	SV:	to be flourishing
fāguāng	～光	VO:	to shine, radiate light
fāmíng	～明	V:	to invent
fāshēng	～生	V:	to happen, occur
fāqǐ	～起	V:	to start (something)
fāxiàn	～现	V:	to discover
fāyuándì	～源地	N:	place of origin, "cradle"
fāyuán	～源	V/N:	to originate, origin
fāzhǎn	～展	V:	to expand, extend, develop
fǎlǜ (lǜfǎ)	法律	N:	law
fǎguān	～官	N:	judge

fān   翻   V: to translate
  fānchulai ～出来 RV: to translate
  fānyì   ～译   V: to translate
fánshì   凡是   PH: all that are
fǎn-   反   •V: to oppose
  fǎndào   V: to make counterproposal
  fǎnduì   ～对   V: to oppose
  fǎndòng   ～动   N: reaction, reactionary
  fǎnkàng   ～抗   V: to oppose, resist
  fánzhèng(fǎnzhèng) MA: in any case
fāng   方   SV: to be square
  fāngfǎ   ～法   N: method
  fāngxiàng ～向   N: aspect, phase
fángbei   防备   V: to prevent
fáng(zi)   房   N: house
  fángdǐng   ～顶   N: roof (of house)
  fángqiáng ～墙   N: wall (of house)
fàng   放   V: to place, put
  fànggěi   ～给   V: to release, put, make
  fàng jiàn ～箭   VO: to shoot an arrow
  fàngqì   ～弃   V: to drop, give up
  fàngxīn   ～心   SV: to be free from anxiety, at
fēizi   妃子   N: imperial concubine
  Guìfēi   贵～   N: "Noble concubine"
féi   肥   SV: to be fat, fleshy (animals,
                           things)
fèi   费   V: to expend, cast aside,
                           remove
  fèichú   废除   V: to abrogate (a treaty)
  fèi shì   费事   VO: to waste effort
fēn   分   V: to divide
  fēnchéng   ～成   V: to divide into, separate
  fēndé   ～得   V: to acquire by division
  fēnjiè   ～界   N: boundary, dividing line
  fēnkāi   ～开   V: to separate, divide
  fēnpèi   ～配   V/N: to apportion, distribute;
                           distribution
  fēnwéi   ～为   V: to divide into
  fēnzuò   ～作   V: to divide or separate into

fēn   纷   SV: confused, numerous, profuse
  fēnzhēng   ～争   V: to dispute, quarrel

fènzi   份子   N: element

fēng   封   V: to officially appoint
  fēngjian zhìdu   N: feudal system, feudalism

fēngsu   风俗   N: custom

fóxiàng   佛像   N: image of Buddha

fūqī   夫妻   N: husband and wife

fūyan   敷衍   SV: to be negligent

fúcóng   服从   V: to obey

fúlǔ   俘虏   N: prisoner of war

fúzhu   扶助   V: to support
  fúzhe   扶着   V: to support, lean on

fǔbài   腐败   V: corrupt

fùnǚ   妇女   N: woman

fùxīng   复兴   V: to revice
  fùxīngqilai   V: to resurrect

fùyú   富裕   V: to be left over
  yǒu fùyú   VO: there is a surplus

fùzá   复杂   SV: to be complicated, complex

fùzé (ren)   责债   VO/SV: to take responsibility;
                              be responsible
fùzǐ   父子   N: father and son

G

gǎi   改   V: to change
  gǎibiàn   ～变   V/N: to change (suddenly);change
  gǎibuliǎo ～不了 RV: to be unable to change
  gǎichéng ～成   V: to change into
  gǎiliáng ～良   V: to improve,change for better
  gǎigé   ～革   V/N: to reform; reform
  gǎiwéi   ～为   V: to change into
  gǎizào   ～造   V: to reform, reconstruct
  gǎizhèng ～正   RV: to correct, revise
  gǎizuò   ～过   V: to change into

gài   盖   V: to build
   gài fáng(zi)   VO: to build a house

gǎn   赶   V: to drive, catch up, hurry
   gǎnchu(qu) ～出 RV: to drive out, expel
   gǎnshang   ～上 RV: to catch up with, happen on

gǎnqíng   感情   N: relation (between parties)

gāngyào   纲要   N: outline, brief sketch

gāngzài   刚才   TW: just recently

gāodao   高到   V: to rise to

gāoliàng   ～梁   N: tall millet, grain sorghum

gé   隔   V: to separate
   měi gé jǐshi lǐ   PH: every few tens of li.

gémìng   革命   V/N: to rebel, revolt; revolution

gēnji   根基   N: root, foundation
   shùgen(r) 树根 N: root of a tree
   gēnběn   根本 MA: fundamentally, at first
gēngdì   耕地   VO: to till fields, plow
gēngtián   ～田   VO: to till fields, plow

gēnggǎi   更改   V: to change, alter

gōng-   公   °N: public, open to all
   gōngchǎn ～产 N: public property
   gōngháng ～行 N: business firm, Cohong
   gōngpíng ～平 SV: to be fair, just
   gōngshǐ ～使 N: ambassador
   gōngtián ～田 N: public lands
   gōngwén ～文 N: official communication
   gōngyòng ～用 V/N: to use publicly, public use

gōng   工   N: labor, job, time
   gōngrén ～人 N: laborer, workman
   gōngshāngyè   N: business and labor
   gōngtóu ～头 N: foreman
   gōngyè ～业 N: industry
   gōngyì ～艺 N: technology
   gōngzuò ～作 N: work, accomplishment

gōng   攻   V: to attack, work at
   gōngdǎ ～打 V: to attack

gōng (cont.)

gōngjī   攻击   V/N: to attack, attack
gōngjìn   ～进   V: to drive into, invade

gōng   宫   N: palave, temple
gōngdiàn   ～殿   N: palace
huánggōng 皇～   N: imperial palace

gōng   功   N: merit, results
gōngxiào   ～效   N: results, fruits

gòng   共   °N: all, whole, to share
gòngchǎn   ～产   VO: to communize property
gòngchǎnzhǔyi N: communism
gòngtóngde ～同的 N: general, universal

gòng   贡   V: to offer as tribute
gòngxiàn   ～献   N: contribution (not monetary)
jìngòng   进～   V: to become tributary

gútou (gǔtou) 骨头 N: bone

gǔ   鼓   N: drum

gǔ   古   SV: to be ancient
gǔwén   ～文   N: ancient literature
cf: lǎo, jiù

gùwèn   顾问   N: advisor

gùyìde   故意地 MA: deliberately, on purpose

guā fēng   刮风   VO: to blow, be windy
guāqi fēng(lai) RV: to blow up a wind, gust

guān   关   N: frontier pass, close
Shānhǎiguān   N: Shanhaikuan (pass between
           山海关   mountains and sea)
guānyú   ～于   CV: concerning, about

guān   官   N: official
guānzhǎng ～长   N: head official
guānzhì   ～制   N: system of officials
guānliáozhǔyi   N: bureaucracy

guánlǐ (guǎnlǐ)   V: to regulate, mamage, control

guàn   灌   V: to pour into, fill up
guàngài   ～溉   N: irrigation
guàn shuǐ ～水   VO: pour water, fill with water

guāngróng 光荣   SV: to be glorious, resplendent

guī	归	V:	to return, revert, belong to
guīshùn	～顺	V:	to go over to, join
guīdìng	规定	V:	to decide, enact, stipulate
guì	跪	V:	to kneel
guìxia	～下	V:	to kneel down
guìzú(rén)	贵族	N:	noble, nobility
mínzú	民族	N:	common people
guó	国	N:	nation, country, state
guódū	～都	N:	national capital
guóhào	～号	N:	dynastic name
guójìde	～际的	N:	international
guójiā	～家	N:	state, nation
guójiè	～界	N:	national boundaries
guójiào	～教	N:	state religion
guólì	～力	N:	national power
guómín	～民	N:	the people
guónèi	～内	PW:	within the country, domestic
guóqí	～旗	N:	national flag
guózhèng	～政	N:	government (abstract)
Guózǐjian	～子监	N:	Hall of the Classics, Beijing

H

hǎi	海	N:	sea
hǎiàn	～岸	N:	seashore
háidǎo(hǎidǎo)		N:	island
hǎidào	～盗	N:	pirate
hǎidào	～道	N:	sea route
hǎijūn	～军	N:	navy
háihǒu(hǎikǒu)		N:	port, seaport
háishuǐ(hǎishuǐ)		N:	sea water
hài	害	V:	to harm, suffer from
hàipà	～怕	V:	to fear, feel afraid
cf: pà, kǒngpà			
hàisǐ	～死	RV:	to do to death, kill
xiānghài	相害	V:	to harm each other
hàn-guó		N:	khanate, state
hànzāi	旱灾	N:	drought
hánghǎi	航海	VO:	to navigate, sail the sea
hǎo róngyi	好容易	SV:	with difficulty

hǎozài	好在	MA:	fortunately
hé	和	SV:	to be in harmony, accord
Dà Hé	大和	N:	early name for Japan
hémù	～睦	SV:	to be agreeable
hépíng	～平	SV:	to be peaceful
hé	合	V:	to join, unite
liánhé	联～	V:	to join, unite
hédī	河堤	N:	dike, levee
héshang	和尚	N:	Buddhist priest, bonze
dàoshi	道士	N:	Taoist priest
láodào	老道	N:	Taoist priest
hèxǐ	贺喜	VO:	to congratulate
hēian	黑暗	N:	darkness
Hēian Shídài		N:	Dark Ages
hèn	恨	V/N:	to hate; grievance
hóngshuǐ(hǒngshuǐ)		N: flood	
hòu	后	N:	rear, previous
hòubànqī	～半期	N:	latter half of a period
cf: qiánbànqī		N:	earlier half of a period
hòuqī	～期	N:	latter period, latter half
hòurén	～人	N:	descendant
hūlōngde		A:	rumblingly (onomatopoetic)
hùxiāng	互相	A:	mutually
hùtiǎr	蝴蝶儿	N:	butterfly
huàjiā	画家	N:	artist
huàixiaqu	坏下去	V:	to deteriorate
huàn-guān	宦官	N:	eunuch
huáng	皇	•N:	imperial
huángzú	～族	N:	imperial clan, family
huángdì	～帝	N:	emperor
huanghòu	～后	N:	empress
huángwèi	～位	N:	imperial throne
huànhuē		VO:	to exchange ratifications
huīfu	恢复	V:	to revert

Huíhui   回回   N: Moslem, Mohammedan
  Huíhuiguó ~ ~国 N: Islamic Empire
  Huíjiào ~ 教 N: Islam

huǐhuài 毀坏、 V: to destroy (from without)

huódong 活动 SV/V: to be active

huózibǎn ~字板 N: printing from movable type

Huǒjiào 火教 N: Mazdaism, fire worship

huǒyào   火药 N: gunpowder

J

jīguān   机关 N: organization

jīhuāng 饥荒 N: famine

jí   极   A: very, extremely
  jídiǎn ~ 点 N: extremity, the limit
  jílìde ~ 力地 MA: promptly, immediately
  jídàde ~大地 N: the largest

jízhōng 集中 V/N: to centralize; centraliza-
                  tion

jǐhé   几何 N: geometry

jì(xia)(lai) V: to set down, record
  jì(lu) 记录 N: record, diary

jì   计   N: stratagem
  jìhua   ~划 N: plan
  jìsuan ~算 V: to calculate

jìxù   继续 V: continue
  jìwèi   ~位 VO: to succeed to the throne

jìyuán   纪元 N: the beginning of an era
  jìyuanhòu   TW: A.D.
  jìyuanqián   TW: B.C.

jiā   加   V: to add
  jiārù   ~入 V: to join (a group), enter

jiā   家   •N: suffix indicating a special-
                  ist,(English -er)
  Dàojiā 道~ N: Taoist
  Fǎjiā   法~ N: Legalist
  káogǔxuéjiā N: archaeologist

jiā (cont.)

lìshijiā	历史~	N:	historian
Mòjiā	墨家	N:	Mohist
Rújiā	儒家	N:	Confucianist
shūjiā		N:	calligrapher
zhéxuejiā		N:	philosopher
zhèngzhijiā		N:	statesman, politician

jiā	家	N:	family, home
jiājuàn	~闺	N:	family group, wife and children
jiāhuo	家伙	N:	utensil
jiāxibiǎo		N:	genealogical chart

jiǎ	假	SV:	to be false
jiáshǐ		V:	even if, falsely assuming
jiǎyì	~意	V:	to pretend

jià(r)	价	N:	price
jiàqián	~钱	N:	price
jiàzhi	~值	N:	value, worth

jiān-ài	兼爱	N:	universal love

jiǎn	减	V:	to subtract, take away
jiánshǎo	~少	V:	to decrease, reduce
jiánshěng	俭省	V:	to be thrifty, economical

jiàn	箭	N:	arrow
fàng jiàn	放~	VO:	to shoot arrows

jiànduì	舰队	N:	navy, fleet

jiàn	建	V:	to establish, build
jiànlì	~立	V:	to establish, set
jiànzào	~造	V:	to build
jiànzhú	~筑	V/N:	to build; architecture

jiāng	江	N:	river
jiānghé	~河	N:	rivers (collective)

jiǎng	讲	V:	to expound, argue, discuss
jiǎnghé	~和	V:	to make peace, reach agreement
jiǎngmíng	~明	V:	to explain clearly

jiàng	将	N:	military general officer
jiàngguān	~官	N:	general officer
jiàngjūn	~军	N:	general, commander

jiāo	浇	V:	to water, sprinkle
jiāoguàn	～灌	V:	to irrigate
jiāo	交	V:	to join, unite, deliver
jiāogěi	～给	V:	to entrust to, hand over
jiāoji	～际	N:	relations, association
jiāoqing	～清	N:	to complete payment(on debt)
jiāoshè	～涉	V/N:	to negotiate; negotiation
jiāotōng	～通	N:	traffic, communications
jiāoyì	交易	V/N:	to trade; commerce
jiāozai	～在	V:	to deliver to, entrust to
jiàozuò	叫作	V:	to call, be called
jiào	教	N:	doctrine, sect
jiàohuì	～会	N:	church, religious group
jiàoshi	～师	N:	teacher
jiàotáng	～堂	N:	church
jiàotú	～徒	N:	follower of a sect,believer
jiàoxun	～训	V/N:	to instruct; teachings
guójiào	国～	N:	state religion
jiēzhe	接着	V:	skipping, every so many
jiēliánzhe	～连着	A:	in a series, on heels of
jiēji	阶级	N:	grade, class
jiéyì	结义	N:	oath (táoyuán sānjiéyì)
jiěmèi	姐妹	N:	sisters (older and younger)
jiěshi	解释	V:	to explain, unravel
jiějué	～决	V:	to solve (a problem)
jiè	借	V:	to borrow
jièyòng	～用	V:	to borrow for use
jièzhe	～着	CV:	by the use of, taking advantage of
jīnyín	金银	N:	gold and silver
jǐnjí	紧急	SV:	to be urgent
jǐnjíde shihou		N:	crisis
jìn	进	°V:	to enter, go forward
jìnbīng	～兵	VO:	to send an armed force
jìnbù	～步	VO/SV:	to make progress, be progressive

jìn (cont.)

jìngòng	进攻	V:	pledge allegiance, pay tribute
jìn guān	～关	V:	enter the pass, cross border
jìnkǒushuì		N:	import duty
jìnjīng	～京	VO:	to go to the capital

jìn	近	SV:	to be near
jìndài	～代	TW:	recent times
jìndaishǐ		N:	recent history, modern times

see dài

jìnzhǐ	禁止	V:	to prohibit
jìnyān	～烟	VO:	to suppress opium

jīng	经	N:	sacred book, classic, sutra
jīngshū	～书	N:	sacred book
jīngyàn	～验	N:	experience
shèngjīng	圣～	N:	Bible
Shū Jing	书～	N:	Book of History
sìjīng	四～	N:	the four classics

jīngcheng	京城	N:	capital city

Jǐngjiào		N:	Nestorian Christianity ("Clear Religion")

jīngměi		SV:	to be beautiful (wén)
jīngměi wú bǐ de		PH:	incomparably beautiful

jiúděng	九等	N:	nine grades (of officialdom)

jùjí	聚集	V:	to gather together, assemble

juéduì	绝对	A:	absolutely

juédìng	决定	V:	to decide
juéduàn	～断	N:	decision

jūn	军	•N:	military, army
jūnduì	～队	N:	army
jūnfèi	～费	N:	military expense
jūnguān	～官	N:	military officer
jūnjiàn	～舰	N:	warship
jūnliáng	～粮	N:	military grain supply
jūnshǐ	～士	N:	soldier
jūnshì	～事	N:	military affairs
lùjūn	陆～	N:	army
hǎijūn	海～	N:	navy
jūnquán	～权	N:	monarchical power

K

kāi	开	V:	to begin, open, found
kāibàn	~办	V:	to initiate, start to do
kāibude	~不得	RV:	should not be started
kāi chuán	~船	VO:	to row a boat
kāidao	~到	RV:	to propel (row) to
kāi guó	~国	VO:	to found a state
kāihua	~化	SV:	to be civilized
kāihuí	~会	V:	to propel back
kāishǐ	~始	V:	to begin
kāi zhàng	~伏	VO:	to start a war
kàn	看	V:	to look, read
kànbuqǐ	~不起	RV:	to look down upon, scorn
kàndao	~到	RV:	to realize
kànfǎ	~法	N:	viewpoint
kǎo	考	V:	to investigate, study, examine
kǎochá	~上	V/N:	to investigate; investigation
káogǔ(kǎo gǔ)		VO:	to study antiquity
káoguxué(jiā)		N:	archaeology, (-ist)
kǎoshang	~上	RV:	to pass examination
kǎoshì	~试	N:	examination
kào	靠	V:	to lean on, rely on
kàodezhù		SV:	to be reliable
kàojìn	~近	V:	to lie near to, be near
kěkào	可~	SV:	to be reliable
kē (kè)	刻	V:	to carve, sculpt
diāokē	雕~	V/N:	to carve; sculpture
kē (mù)bǎn		VO:	to carve blocks(for print)
kēxué	科学	N:	science
kěhàn	可汗	N:	khan (ruler's title)
kě (kéyi)	可	AV:	to be able, to be permissible
kějiàn	~见	SV:	it can be seen that
kězuò	~作	SV:	to be permissible
kēng	坑	N:	pit (vertical)
cf: dòng	洞	N:	cave (horizontal)

kǒu	口	N:	mouth, opening, port
kǒuàn	～岸	N:	port
kǒuhào	～号	N:	motto, battlecry, slogan
háikǒu	海～	N:	seaport
hékǒu	河～	N:	mouth of a river
kōng	空	SV:	to be empty, vacant
kōng huà	～语	N:	empty talk, idle talk
kōng chéng jì		N:	strategem of the empty city
kuàilè	快乐	SV/N:	to be happy; happiness
kuān	宽	SV:	to be wide, broad, loose
kùnnan	困难	SV/N:	to be difficult; hardship

L

lái	来	V:	to come
láibují	～不及	SV:	there isn't time to do it
láiwǎng	～往	N:	intercourse, coming and going
lǎo	老	SV:	to be old
lǎobǎixìng		N:	the common people
lǎodà	～大	N:	the eldest son (or brother)
lǎoèr	～二	N:	the second son (or brother)
láohǔ	～虎	N:	tiger
lǎoruò	～弱	SV:	to be old and infirm
lǎosān	～三	N:	third son (or brother)
lǎoshi	～实	SV:	to be tractable, good-tempered
lào(or luò)	落	V:	to fall, drop, (sun) set
lēisǐ	勒死	RV:	to strangle, choke to death
léi	雷	N:	thunder
dǎléi	打～	VO:	to thunder
lì	立	V:	to set up, establish
lìguó	～国	VO:	to found a state
lìxiànguó		N:	constitutional state
jiànlì	建立	V:	to establish
lì	力	N:	strength, power
lìliang	～量	N:	strength, force, authority
cf: shìli, quánbing, jìn			
lì(zi)	例	N:	example
lìrú	～如	V:	take for example

lì	利	N:	advantage, benefit
lì-hài	～害	N:	good and ill, benefit and injury
lìyòng	～用	V:	to make use of
lì	历	V/N:	undergo; calendar
lìfǎ	～法	N:	calendar calculation, astronomy
lìshǐ	～史	N:	history
lìshǐjiā	～史家	N:	historian
lián	联	•V:	to join, unite
liánjūn	～军	N:	allied army
liánluò	～络	V:	to make contact with
liánnián	连年	TW:	year after year
liánqilai		RV:	join, connect
liànbīng	练兵	VO:	train troops
liáng	粮	N:	grain
liángshi(shíliáng)		N:	grain
liángmǐ(mǐliáng)		N:	grain and rice, grains
liǎng	两	M:	ounce, tael (silver)
lín	邻	•V:	to be near
línguó	～国	N:	neighboring country
línjìn	～近	SV:	to be contiguous, near
línjù	～居	N:	neighbor
línshí	临时	A:	temporarily
líng	陵	N:	imperial tomb
lǐngshi	领事	N:	consul
lǐngshiguǎn		N:	consulate
lǐngshi-cáipan-quán		N:	consular jurisdiction, extra-territoriality
lǐng	领	V:	to lead, receive
lǐngshòu	～受	V:	to receive
lǐngtǔ (lǐng-tǔ)		N:	territory (possession)
lǐngxiù	～袖	N:	leader
lìng	另	SP:	other, different (usually before yi)
lìngwài	～外	SP/A:	in addition, besides
liúxia	留下	RV:	to keep, retain, leave behind

liú	流	V/N:	to flow, wander; •flow, stream, current
liúyù	~域	N:	river valley, basin, course
lǒngluò	笼络	V:	to gather in, attract
lùxù(de)	陆续	MA:	one by one, one after another
luòtuó	骆驼	N:	camel
lüxíng	旅行	V/N:	to travel; travels
lüxingjiā		N:	traveler
lüxingjì		N:	travelog, record of travel

M

mǎbīng	马兵	N:	cavalry, horseman
máo	毛	N/M:	hair, fur, feathers; dime
máobing	~病	N:	flaw
máoqián	~钱	N:	subsidiary currency, dimes
māo (mō)	摸	V:	to feel, reach, grope for
māobuzháo		RV:	cannot get, cannot secure
měi	美	SV:	to be beautiful
měide	~德	N:	great virtue
měishù	~术	N:	arts, fine arts
mén	门	M:	for cannon
mǐ	米	N:	rice, grain
mǐfàn	~饭	N:	cooked rice
mǐjià	~价	N:	the price of rice
dàmǐ	大~	N:	rice
xiǎomǐ	小~	N:	millet
mìmì	秘密	N:	secret
miàn	面	N:	surface, face, side
miào	庙	N:	temple (usually Buddhist)
miè	灭	V:	to extinguish
mièwáng	~亡	V/N:	to perish; fall (of a state or dynasty
xiāomiè	消灭	V:	to extinguish, wipe out
mín	民	N:	people
rénmín	人~	N:	people, all the people, everyone

mín (cont.)

   mínjūn ～军 N: people's army, revolution-
      ary army
   mínzú ～族 N: tribe, race

míng(zi) 名 N: name, fame
   míngrén ～人 N: famous person
   míngyi ～义 N: authority, title
   míngyu ～誉 N: fame, reputation

mìng 命 N: fate, decree
   mìngling ～令 N: decree, official order
   fā (or xià) mìngling VO: to issue a decree
   zūn(shǒu) mìngling VO: to obey a mandate

mò 末 SP: the last
   mòcì ～次 N: the last time
   mòhòu ～后 TW: at last, finally
   mòliǎo(r) ～了 A: finally
   mònián ～年 N: the last year, final years
   mòqī ～期 N: the last period, latter
      part of a period
   mòwěi ～尾 N: the end, at the last
   Míngmò 明末 TW: the close of the Ming
      dynasty

mófàn 模范 N: pattern
   mófǎng VO: to imitate, follow pattern

mǒu 某 SP: a certain (indefinite)

mùbǎn 木板 N: wooden block or boasd

mùbīng 募兵 VO: recruit soldiers
   mùbīngzhì N: voluntary enlistment
   cf: zhēngbīngzhì N: conscription

mùdi 目的 N: purpose, aim

N

názhùle 拿住了 RV: to seize (securely)

nà shuì 纳税 VO: to pay taxes

nánjìn 南进 V: to drive southward (mil.)

nántí 难题 N: problem, difficult question

nào 闹 V: to disturb, make a fuss
   nào shuǐzāi VO: to have floods
   nào túfěi VO: to be plagued by bandits

nèiluàn　内乱　N:　internal disturbance, civil war

néng　能　AV:　to be able to
　nénggou　～够　AV:　to be able to
　néngli　～力　N:　ability
　nénggàn　～干　SV:　to be capable, talented

nián　年　N:　year
　niándai　～代　N:　duration, length of years
　niánhào　～号　N:　reign title of an emperor
　niánhuì　～会　N:　annual meeting, kuriltai-(Mongol)
　niántou(r)　～头　N:　harvest, crop

nóng　农　N:　agriculture
　nóngfu　～夫　N:　farmer
　nóngmín　～民　N:　farmers (collectively)
　nóngren　～人　N:　farmer
　nóngyè　～业　N:　farming, agriculture

nǚ　女　SV:　to be female
　nǚ guān　～官　N:　female official
　nǚxu　～婿　N:　son-in-law, daughter's husband
nüedài　虐待　V:　to mistreat, persecute

P

páchulai　爬出来　RV:　climb out, crawl out

páizhǎng　排长　N:　platoon commander

páiwài(de)　～外　VO:　anti-foreign

pài　派　V:　to send, detail
　pàibīng　～兵　VO:　to detail soldiers

pángguān　旁观　V:　to look on from the side

pào　炮　N:　cannon (M: mén)

péi　赔　V:　to pay damages
　péikuǎn　～款　VO/N:　to pay indemnity, indemnity

pèifu　佩服　V:　to approve, respect, admire

pèng dīngzi　碰钉子　VO:　"strike a nail", meet an obstacle

pī　匹　M:　measure for horses

pīping	批评	V:	to criticize
piān	篇	M:	for poems, literary works
shīpiān	诗～	N:	Psalms
pǐnxíng	品行	N:	character, disposition
píng	平	SV:	to be level, peaceful
píngān		SV/N:	to be peaceful; peace
píngděng	～等	SV:	to be equal, on the same level in the same class
píngdìng	～定	V:	to "pacify", put down rebellion
pínglùn	评论	N:	editorial
píngmín	～民	N:	common people

Q

qī	期	°N:	period of time
qiánqī	前～	N:	earlier period or part of period
hòuqī	后～	N:	later period or part of period
shíqī	时～	N:	period, era
qīfu	欺负	V:	to harass, take advantage
qīpian	～骗	V:	to cheat
shòu qīpian		VO:	to get cheated
qí	其	PN:	(literary) his, hers, its
qízhōng	～中	PW:	in the midst of it
qíyú	～余	N:	the rest, the remaining
qǐ	起	V:	to start, begin
qǐ bīng	～兵	VO:	to raise an army
qǐdiǎn (qǐ)	～点	N:	starting point
qǐ máfan	～麻烦	VO:	to start trouble, stir up
qǐ míngzi	～名子	VO:	to give a name to
qǐshǐ (qǐ)	～始	TW:	at the outset
qǐtóu(r)	～头	MA:	at the outset
qǐyuán	～源	N:	origin, source
qì	气	V/N:	to anger, become angry; anger
qìjù	器具	N:	tool, implement
qiàqiǎo	恰巧	MA:	by luck
qiān	迁	V:	to remove
qiāndào	～到	V:	to remove (capital) to
qiāndū	～都	VO:	to remove the capital

qiānzì	签字	VO:	to sign (letter, document, treaty)
qiānlímǎ	千里马	N:	horse that could travel 1000 lĭ in a day
qiánqĭ	前期	N:	the earlier period
qiándài	~代	N:	a former period
qiánhòu	~后	TW:	from first to last, altogether
qiánxiān	~线	N:	front lines (military)
qiánliáng	钱粮	N:	tax
qiāngpào	枪炮	N:	firearms
qiáng	强	SV:	to be strong
qiángdào	~盗	N:	robber, bandit
qiáng guó	~国	VO:	to strengthen the state
qiángshèng	~盛	SV:	to be prosperous, strong
qiángzhuàng	~壮	SV:	to be strong, sturdy
qiǎng	抢	V:	to seize, take by force
qiǎngguolai	抢过来	RV:	seize, take over to one's own side
qiǎngpò	强迫	V:	to force, compel
qiǎngqu	抢去	RV:	to take away
qiǎngxiān	~先	VO:	to strive for first place
qiáo	瞧	V:	to see
qiáo nĭde	~你的	VO:	it's up to you
qiáoliáng	桥梁	N:	bridge timber, span, step (toward objective)
qiáomín	侨民	N:	emigrant
qīnchāi	钦差	N:	ambassador, personal envoy
qīnzì	亲目	N:	in-person, oneself
qīn	侵	°V:	to attack
qīnlüè	~略	V/N:	to attack, invade; attack
qīnzhàn	~占	V:	to occupy militarily
qín	琴	N:	musical instrument (stringed)
tánqín	弹~	VO:	to play a (stringed) musical instrument
qĭngyuàn	请愿	V/N:	to petition; petition
qióngkŭ	穷苦	SV:	to be poor
qŭqī	娶妻	VO:	to take a wife

qǔxiāo	取消	V:	to eliminate, do away with
quán	全	SV:	to be entire; entirely, completely, all
quánguó	～国	N:	the entire nation
quánbù	～部	N:	the entire region
quándōu	～都	A:	entirely, completely
quánquán	～权	N:	full power, plenipotentiary
quánlì	权力	N:	power
quàn	劝	V:	to plead, implore, urge
quēshǎo	缺少	V:	to lack, be wanting
qúndǎo	群岛	N:	a group of islands, archipelago

R

ráner	然而	A:	but, and yet
ránhòu	～后	TW:	thereafter
ràng	让	V:	to give in, yield
réqilai(rě)		RV:	to arouse, stir up
rén	人	N:	man, person, people
rénshu	～数	N:	population
rénxíng	～性	N:	human nature
rénwù	～物	N:	human figure, statuette
rěn	忍	V:	to be patient, put up with
rèn	认	V:	to acknowledge
rènzhēn	～真	SV:	to be honest
rènwéi	～为	V:	to regard as, consider
réngrán	仍然	A:	still, persistently
rì	日	N:	sun, day
Rìběn	～本	N:	Japan, Land of the Rising Sun
Rìchūchù	～出处	N:	early name for Japan, sunrise place
rìcháng	～常	SV:	daily
rónghé	融合	V:	to blend, mix, amalgamate
ròulei	肉类	N:	belong to the meat category

rú   如   V: for instance, such as
　rútóng   ～同   V: to be like, similar to

rùjiào   入教   VO: to join a church

ruò   弱   SV: to be weak, weaken
　ruòdiǎn   ～点   N: weakness, weak point
　shuāiruò 衰弱   V: to weaken, degenerate

<u>S</u>

Sānguó Zhǐ Yǎnyi N: Story of the Three Kingdoms

sǎo   扫   V: to sweep
　sǎodì   ～地   VO: to sweep the floor or ground

shāmò   沙漠   N: desert
　shāmòdi   ～～地   N: desert
　Dà Shāmò 大～～   N: Gobi Desert

shāndòng   山洞   N: cave

shāng   商   °N: trade, business, commerce
　shānghǎng ～行   N: business firm, Cohong
　shānglü   ～旅   N: merchant, trader
　shāngye   ～业   N: commerce, trade
　tōngshāng 通～   VO: to carry on trade

shāng   伤   V: to wound, harm
　shānghài ～害   V: to harm
　shāngxīn ～心   VO: to grieve, be grieved

shǎng(gěi)(shǎng)   V: to bestow, donate

shàngdàng   上当   VO: to get cheated

shàngxià   上下   SV: to be more or less, about

shǎoshù   少数   N: minority

shēchi   奢侈   SV: to be extravagant, wasteful

shè(lì)   设   V: to build, establish

shèhuì   社会   N: society
　shèhuixué   N: sociology
　shèhuijiā   N: sociologist

shēn   身   N: body, self
　shēntǐ   ～体   N: body, health
　shēnshang ～上   PW: on the body

shēn (cont.)
  qīnshēn　亲身　N:　personally, oneself
  miè jiā wáng shēn　PH:　end the family line and
                    destroy one's self

shēng　生　V:　beget, produce
  shēng bīng　～病　VO:　to get sick
  shēngchǎn　～产　V:　to produce
  shēnghuó　～活　N:　livelihood, way of living
  shēngjì　～计　N:　livehood
  shēngmìng　～命　N:　life existence

shěngjiè　省界　N:　provincial boundary

shēngkou　牲口　N:　draft animals

shèng　胜　SV:　to be victorious
  shèngguo　～过　V:　to gain a victory over,
                  conquer
  shèngzhàn　N:　victory

shèng　圣　SV:　to be sacred
  shèngjīng　～经　N:　sacred scripture, Bible
  shèngrén　～人　N:　holy man, sage

shèngxia　剩下　RV:　to remain over, be left over

shèng　盛　SV:　abundant, energetic

shī　诗　N:　poem
  shījiā　～家　N:　poet
  Shījīng　～经　N:　Book of Odes
  shīrén　～人　N:　poet

shībài　失败　V:　to be defeated,lose a fight

shíxíng　实行　V:　to carry out,give effect to

shízì　识字　VO:　learn to read, be literate

shí　石　•N:　stone
  shíqì　～器　N:　stone tool
  shíxiàng　～像　N:　stone image

shí　时　•N:　time
  shídài　～代　N:　period (of time), age
  shíjian　～间　N:　time, period of time

shí　实　•SV:　to be real, true
  shílì　～力　N:　real power　(cf.: shìli)
  shíxiàn　～现　V:　to realize, put into effect

shíliáng(liángshi)　N:grain
  食粮

shíyè	家业	N:	industry
shǐ	使	CV:	to use, send, commission, cause to
shǐchén	使臣	N:	ambassador, diplomatic emissary
shǐguǎn	使馆	N:	legation
shǐyòng	使用	V:	to use
shǐ	史	N:	history
shǐshū	～书	N:	work of history, historical writing
Shǐjì	～记	N:	Record of History
shìchǎng	市场	N:	market
shìjì	世纪	N:	century
shìlì	势力	N:	power (human, governmental)
shìyàng	式样	N:	pattern
shìyòng	适用	SV:	to be suitable, appropriate
shōu	收	V:	to receive
shōudào	～到	V:	to receive
shōuhuilai		RV:	to receive back, get back
shōushuì	～税	VO:	to collect taxes
shóuxi	熟悉	SV:	to be familiar
shǒu	手	N:	hand
shǒuduàn	～段	N:	device, trick
shǒuxià	～下	N:	under one's authority
shǒuxu	～续	N:	process
shǒujiù	守旧	VO:	to be conservative, traditional
shòu	受	V:	to endure, suffer
shòu yǐngxiǎng		VO:	to be affected, influenced
shòubuliao		RV:	cannot bear, unable to endure
shòu gōngjì		VO:	bear (suffer) an attack
shòu kǔ	～苦	VO:	to endure hardship
shòu qīpian		VO:	"get stung", be cheated
shòu sǔnshi		VO:	to suffer harm
shū	书	N:	book
shūjì	～记	N:	scribe, secretary
shūjiā	～家	N:	calligrapher
shūjú	～局	N:	book shop

shúshu	叔々	N:	uncle, father's younger brother
shǔ	数	V:	to count
shǔ	属	V:	to belong to
shǔguó	～国	N:	subject state
shǔyú	～于	V:	to belong to
shùzhī	树枝	N:	tree branch
shùshuō	述说	V:	to discuss, set forth in detail
shuāi	摔	V:	to fall, tumble
shuāiruò	衰弱	V:	to decline, weaken
shuǐ	水	N:	water
shuǐgōu	～沟	N:	irrigation ditch, drainage ditch
shuǐshǒu	水手	N:	sailor, ship hand
shuǐzāi	～灾	N:	flood
shuì	税	N:	tax
shuìfǎ	～法	N:	customs tariff
shuìlì	～吏	N:	tax
nàshuì	纳～	VO:	to pay tax
jìnkǒushuì		N:	import tax
shàngshuì		VO:	to impose tax
shōushuì	收～	VO:	to collect tax
shùncóng	顺从	V:	to follow, go according to
shuō	说	V:	to speak, say
shuōdao	～到	RV:	to mention, speak of
shuōhé	～和	RV:	to bring about agreement, make peace
sīzì	私自	N:	oneself, personally
sìzhōuwéi	四周围	N:	all sides, on all sides
cf.:zhōuwéi, sìwéi		N:	all sides, on all sides
súhuà	俗话	N:	vernacular, common saying
sùxiàng	塑像	VO:	to make a clay image
suànle ba	算了吧	PH:	let it go at that, call it quits
suànxué	算学	N:	mathematics
sūnzi	孙子	N:	grandson (father's side)
sǔnshi	损失	N:	harm, ill-effects

T

tàidu	态度	N:	attitude
tánqín	弹琴	VO:	play a musical instrument (stringed), pluck
táo	逃	V:	sneak
táozǒu	～走	V:	to steal away, sneak away
táodao	～到	V:	to escape to
táopǎo	～跑	V:	to run away, escape
táoyuán sānjieyì 桃园三结义		PH:	The Triple Oath of the Peach Garden, blood brotherhood of the three heroes
tǎolun	讨论	V:	to discuss
tào	套	M:	sort, brand
tíchāng	提倡	V:	to promote, advocate
tímu	题目	N:	topic
tiān	天	N:	heaven, day, sky
Tiāndì	～地	N:	Heavenly Younger Brother
Tiānfù	～父	N:	Heavenly Father
tiānwén(xué)		N:	astronomy
tiānxià	～下	N:	all under heaven, the world
Tiānxiōng	～兄	N:	Heavenly Elder Brother
tiānzāi	～灾	N:	natural calamity
Tiānzǐ	～子	N:	Son of Heaven, emperor
Tiānzhǔjiào	～主教	N:	Roman Catholic Church
tiánzhì	田制	N:	land system
tiāo(chulai)	挑	RV:	pick out, select
tiáoyuē	条约	N:	treaty
tiěqì(see qì)		N:	iron tool
tíng	停	V:	to stop
tíngzai	～在	V:	to stop at
tíngzhǐ	～止	V:	to halt, cease operating
tíngzhù	～住	V:	to stop, bring to a halt
tōng	通	V:	to pass through
tōngdao	～到	V:	to go through to, penetrate to
tōngshāng	～商	VO:	to carry on trade
tōngxíng	～行	SV:	to be open to traffic, be current

tōng (cont.)
  tōngyòng 通用 SV:　to be in general use

tóng 铜 N:　bronze, copper
  tóngqì ～器 N:　bronze tool
  tóngqián ～钱 N:　brass cash, coins
  tóngzěr ～子儿 N:　copper coin

tóng 同 ◦V:　together, united
  tónghuà ～化 V:　to assimilate, blend
  tóngshí ～时 A:　at the same time
  tóngxìng ～性 SV:　to have the same surname
  tóngxué ～学 N:　schoolmate, fe-low student

tǒng 统 ◦N:　all, general, gather
  tǒngyī ～一 V:　unify, unite
  tǒngyīqilai RV:　to unify
  tǒngzhì ～治 V:　to govern, rule
  tǒngzhì V:　to control
  (dà) zóngtǒng N:　president (national)
  chéng yìtǒng VO:　to come under one rule

tóuxiáng 投降 V:　to surrender

tú 图 N:　map, chart, picture
  túshuguǎn N:　library
  dìtú 地～ N:　map

tǔ 土 N:　earth, native
  tǔrén ～人 N:　native
  tǔshān ～山 N:　hill, mound
  tǔwù ～物 N:　native product, indigenous
           product

tuán 团 N:　group, organization
  tuánjié ～结 V:　to affiliate, cohere
  tuántǐ ～体 N:　group, body
  Yìhétuán 义和～ N:　Righteous Fist Society,
           Boxers

tuī 推 V:　to push
  tuīfān ～翻 V:　to overthrow

tuì 退 V:　to retire
  tuìbīng ～兵 VO:　to withdraw troops
  tuìwèi ～位 VO:　to abdicate

tuó 驮 V:　to carry on the back (of
           animals)

  cf.: V:　to carry on the back (of man)

W

wā	挖	V:	to dig, scoop out
wāchulai		RV:	to dig out
wā kēng	～坑	VO:	to dig a pit
wài	外	•N:	outside, foreign
wàijiāo	～交	N:	foreign relations
wàizú	～族	N:	alien race
wánchéng	完成	V:	to complete, bring to completion
wángwèi	王位	N:	royal throne, princely rank
wáng	亡	•V:	perish
wángguó	～国	VO:	to destroy the nation
mièwáng	灭～	V:	to perish
wǎnglái	往来	N:	coming and going, intercourse
wéi	围	V:	to surround
wéizai	～在	V:	to surround in
wéixīn	维新	V:	to reform
wén	文	•N:	literary, civil
wénhua	～化	N:	civilization, culture
wénlǐ		N:	classical literary style
wénmíng	～明	SV:	to be cultured, civilized
wénrén	～人	N:	scholar literatus
wénshèngrén		N:	civil sage
wénxué	～学	N:	literature
wénxuéshǐ		N:	history of literature
wénzhāng	～章	N:	essay, composition
wénzì	～字	N:	written characters, writings
běnwénde		N:	of the original version
xuéwen	学文	N:	learning
wō	倭	N:	dwarf
Wōnú	～奴	N:	Dwarf slave, Japanese (old)
Wōnúguó	～国	N:	Dwarf Kingdom, Japan (old)
wú	无	V:	<u>negative of</u> to have (literary)
wúbǐ	～比	VO:	to be without peer (lit.)
wúnéng	～能	VO:	to be incapable
wúsuobuwèi	无所不为	PH:	there's nothing he doesn't do
wúsuowèi	无所为	PH:	there is no such thing, not matter

wǔ	武	•N:	military
wǔgōng	～功	N:	military exploits
wǔlì	～力	N:	military power
wǔqì	～器	N:	military implements, weapons
wǔhuā bāmén	五花八门	PH:	five flowers eight gates - numerous in kind, wide variety
wùzhì	物质	N:	material thing, goods

X

xí	习	•V:	to practice
xíguàn	～惯	N:	habit
xísù	～俗	N:	habit and custom, tradition
liànxí	练习	V:	to practice
xì	戏	N:	drama, play
xìjiā	～家	N:	dramatist, player
xìjù	～剧	N:	a play, drama
xìshén	～神	N:	god of drama
xìqǔ	～曲	N:	musical play, opera
xì	细	SV:	to be fine, detailed
xìxīrde	～～地	MA:	minutely, meticulously
xiángxì	详～	SV:	to be meticulous
xìtǒng	系统	N:	order, organization
yǒuxìtǒng		VO/SV:	to be orderly, systematic
xià	下	V:	to go down
xiàbù	～部	N:	lower section
xiàliú	～流	N:	lower course (of a river)
xiàluò	～落	N:	hiding place
xià Xīyáng	～西洋	VO:	to sail the Western (Indian) Ocean
xiàzi	～子	M:	a blow of the hand; a time
xià	吓	V:	to frighten
xiàdiàole	～倒了	RV:	scare to the point of dropping something
xiàhu	～唬	V:	to frighten
xiàhuàile	～坏了	RV:	scare to "pieces"
xiānhòu	先后	TW:	before and after, first and last
xiàn	现	•N:	present time
xiànzài	～在	TW:	now
xiàndài	～代	N:	the present time(s)

xiàngěi 献给 V: to give (to a superior), offer to

xiànzhi 限制 V/N: to restrict, restrain; restriction

xiāng 相 V: mutual, reciprocal
  xiāngài ～爱 V: to love each other
  xiāngdāng ～当 SV: to be appropriate
  xiāngtóng ～同 SV: to resemble, be the same
  xiāngxìn ～信 V: to believe in, trust
  xiāngzhēng ～争 V: to quarrel
  hùxiāng 互～ A: mutually

xiángxì 详细 SV: to be detailed, meticulous

xiǎngyìng 响应 V: to echo, be influenced by

xiàng 像 N: image, picture, resemblance
  Fóxiàng 佛像 N: image of Buddha
  ǒuxiàng 偶像 N: image, idol
  shíxiàng 石像 N: stone image

xiàng 象 N: elephant

xiàng 向 CV: toward

xiāomiè 消灭 V: to extinguish, annihilate

xiǎo 小 SV: to be small
  xiǎokàn ～看 V: to look down upon
  xiáomǐ ～米 N: millet
  xiǎo míngr ～名 N: "small name", nickname
  xiǎoshuō ～说 N: novel, story

xiàoguǒ 效果 N: result

xīnlǐ(xué) 心理 N: psychology, mentality

xīn 新 SV: to be new
  xīnshì(de) ～式 N: new fashion(ed)
  xīnxīngde ～兴的 N: newly arisen

xìn 信 V: to believe
  xìnrèn ～任 V: to believe in, trust
  xìnyǎng ～仰 V: to believe in

xīng 兴 °V: to prosper, originate
  xīngqilai RV: to spring up, become strong
  xīngwàng SV: to prosper, be prosperous
  xīnxīngde N: newly arisen

xíng	行	V:	to do, go
xíngzhèng	～政	VO:	to carry on government, administer
xíngshi	形式	N:	shape, appearance
xíngfǎ	刑法	N:	punishment, penalty
xìngzhi	性质	N:	characteristic, quality
xiū	修	V:	to repair
xiūgǎi	～改	V:	to edit, amend
xiūli	～理	V:	to repair
xiū lù	～路	VO:	repair or make a road
xiùshǒu	袖手	VO:	to put hands in sleeves
xùyán	序言	N:	preface, introduction
xuān	宣	V:	to proclaim, publish
xuānchuán	～传	V:	to propagate, preach
xuānyán	～言	N:	proclamation
xuānzhàn	～战	VO:	declare war
xuǎn	选	V:	to select, choose
xuǎnchū	～出	RV:	to pick out
xuánjǔ	～举	V:	to elect
xué	学	V:	to learn, study
xuéshù	～术	N:	scholarship, learning
xuéshuō	～说	N:	theory, school of thought
xuépài	～派	N:	school of thought
xuéwen	～问	N:	learning
xuézhě	～者	N:	scholar
xùnliàn	训练	V:	to train, drill

Y

yāzhi	压制	V:	to oppress
yāpo	～迫	V:	to oppress
yǎpiàn	鸦片	N:	opium
yámen	衙门	N:	official's office
yānsǐ	淹死	RV:	to drown
yán	言	•N:	language
yányǔ(yǔyán)		N:	language
yánlùn	～论	N:	speech, oration, discussion

yǎnguāng 眼光 N: vision, point of view

yàn 沿 V: to lie near
  yànhǎi ～海 VO: to lie near the coast
  yànhé ～河 VO: by the riverside
  héyàn 河～ N: riverbank

yǎng 养 V: to nurture, nourish, keep
  yǎnghuó ～活 V: to keep, raise (animals)
  yǎng cán ～蚕 VO: to raise silkworms

yāoqiú 要求 V: to petition, request(formal)

yáodòng N: movement (socio-political)

yàodiǎn ～点 N: important point

yàoshuǐ 药水 N: medicine (liquid),chemical

yě 野 SV: to be wild, untamed
  yěshòu ～兽 N: wild animal
  yěxīn ～心 SV: to be aggressive, ruthless
  yězhū ～猪 N: wild boar

yīxué 医学 N: the study of medicine

yī 一 NU: one
  yízhì 一致 SV: to be of the same system, similar
  yìtǒng 一同 N: unit, a united whole

yíchu 益处 N: benefit

yíhuo 疑惑 V: to suspect
  yíxīn ～心 N: suspicion

yímín 移民 VO: to migrate
  yírén ～人 N: immigrant

yìchéng 译成 V: translate into

yìhé 议和 V: to make peace

yīnyuèjiā 音乐家 N: musician

yìn 印 V: to print
  yìnshū ～书 VO: to print books
  yìnshuā(shuāyìn) V: to print
  yìnshuāshù ～刷术 N: the art of printing
  yīngyòng 应用 V: the need (to use), be suitable

yíngxiǎng 影响 V/N: to influence; influence,
                              effect
  shòu yíngxiǎng VO: to be influenced
  yǒu yíngxiǎng VO: to have influence

yòng   用   V: to use
  yòngjìn ～尽 RV: to use up, use to the limit
  yòngqilai   RV: to start using, applying

yōudài 优待 V: to treat well
  <u>cf.</u>: nüèdài V: to treat badly

yóumu(rén) 遊牧 N: nomad

yǒu   有   V: to have
  yǒulǐ   VO/SV: to be reasonable, proper
  yǒuqùwei   VO/SV: to be interesting
  yǒu yíngxiǎng VO/SV: to have influence, be
                              affected

yúshuǐ(yǔ) 雨水 N: rain, rainwater

yùzháo   遇着 RV: to meet, contact, happen
                              upon

yùsuàn   预算 V/N: to estimate, to budget;
                              budget

yùn   运   V: to transport
  yùndong ～动 N: a movement (group activity)
  yùnhé ～河 N: canal
  yùnhuò ～货 VO: to transport goods, to ship

yuǎnzhēng 远征 V: to make a military expedi-
                              tion

Z

zāi   灾   N: calamity
  zāihuāng ～荒 N: calamity
  hànzāi 旱灾 N: drought
  shuǐzāi 水～ N: flood

zǎixiàng 宰相 N: premier, prime minister

zài nèi 在内 VO: is included

zāo   糟   SV: to be rotten

zàofǎn   造反 V: to rebel

zàojiǔ   ～酒 VO: to make wine

zào chuán ～船 VO: shipbuilding

zēngjiā 增加 V: to add, increase
  zēngjìn ～进 V: to add, increase

zhàn 站 N: post, station

zhàn 占 V: to occupy
  zhànlǐng ～领 V: to take (mil.), capture

zhànzhēng 战争 N: battle, war, fighting

zhāngcheng 章程 N: regulations

zhǎngguān 长官 N: commanding officer
  guānzhǎng 官长 N: officials, authorities

zhào(zhe) 照 CV: to follow a pattern, according to

zhéxué 哲学 N: philosophy
  zhéxuéjiā N: philosopher

zhèmma yǐlái MA: thus, in this way, and so

zhēnzhèng 真挚 SV: to be genuine

zhēng 争 V: to contest, fight, argue, fight over
  zhēng dìpán VO: to quarrel over territory
  zhēngqilai RV: to start quarreling
  xiāngzhēng V: compete, fight

zhēng 征 V: levy, collect
  zhēngbīng ～兵 VO: to conscript soldiers
  zhēngbingzhì N: conscription
  zhēngshōu ～收 V: to collect by levy
  zhēngshuì ～税 VO: levy taxes
  cf.: shōushuì VO: collect taxes

zhénglǐ 整理 V: to put in order

zhěnggē(r)de N: entire, whole

zhèng 政 •N: government
  zhèngcè ～策 N: governmental policy
  zhèngfǔ ～府 N: government (concrete), the state
  zhèngquán ～权 N: ruling power
  zhèngzhì ～治 N: government (abstract), system of government
  zhèngzhi-gǎigéjiā N: political reformer

zhèng (cont.)
  bànlǐ guózhèng VO: carry on the government
  xíngzhèng 行政 VO: administer the government
  guózhèng 国政 N: national government
zhèngjù 证据 N: evidence, proof
  zhèngmíng ⌣明 V: to prove
zhènghǎo 正好 SV: to be just right, just in time
zhǐbǎichōuwǔ NU: five percent (ad valorem)
zhīpai 支派 N: tribe
zhǐhǎo 只好 V: it would be best to..., I can only...
zhíjiede 直接的 A: directly
zhíye 职业 N: occupation
zhīshi 知识 N: knowledge, wisdom
zhībù 织布 VO: to waeve cloth
zhìqi 志气 N: ambition
zhìdu 制度 N: system
  bìzhì 币制 N: monetary system
  fēngjiàn zhìdu N: feudal system
  tiánzhì 田⌣ N: land system
  zhèngzhì 政制 N: system of government
zhìlǐ 治理 V: to organize, manage
zhōng 钟 N: bell
zhōng 中 •N: middle
  Zhōngguo ⌣国 N: Middle Kingdom, China
  zhōngyāng ⌣央 N: the (administrative) center
  jízhōng 集中 VO: to centralize
zhǒng 种 M: kind, sort, type
  zhǒnglèi ⌣类 N: kind, sort, type
  zhǒngzú ⌣族 N: race, people
  zhǒngzhǒngde SP: all sorts of, every sort of
zhòng 重 SV: weighty, heavy, important
  zhòngdà ⌣大 SV: to be important, major
  zhòngkàn ⌣看 V: to regard highly, respect
  zhòngyào ⌣要 SV: to be important
  zhòngyòng ⌣用 V: to use in an important position

zhōu	洲	N:	continent
Aozhou	澳洲	N:	Australia
Fēizhou	非~	N:	Africa
Měizhou	美~	N:	America (continent)
Ouzhou	欧~	N:	Europe
Yǎzhou	亚~	N:	Asia
zhūhóu	诸侯	N:	feudal prince, lord
zhú(zi)	竹	N:	bamboo
zhúgān(r)	~竿	N:	bamboo pole
zhúpiàn	~片	N:	bamboo slip (ancient writing material)
zhúyi	主意	N:	idea, plan
zhǔ	主	N:	lord, master
zhǔquán	~权	N:	sovereignty
zhǔzhàn	~战	VO:	to advocate making war
zhǔzhāng	~张	V:	to advocate
zhǔyì	~义	N:	doctrine, -ism
zhùzhòng	注重	V:	to stress, emphasize
zhùyì	~意	V:	to pay attention to
zhùxia	住下	V:	to settle down
zhuā	抓	V:	to claw, seize
zhuāzhù	~住	RV:	to seize securely
zhuān	专	SV:	to be a specialist in
		A:	solely
zhuānguǎn	~管	V:	to have sole charge of
zhūanzhì	专制	N:	dictatorship, absolute rule
zhuǎn	转	V:	to turn
zhuǎndao	~到	V:	to turn to
zhuāng	装	V:	to pack, load
zhuāngmǎnle		RV:	filled full (of)
zhuāng chē	~车	VO:	to load a cart
zhuāngjia	庄稼	VO/N:	grow crops; farming, crops
zhuī	追	V:	to pursue
zhuīshang	~上	RV:	to catch up with
zhuīhuilai		RV:	to catch anf bring back
zhǔn	准	V:	to permit, allow
zhǔnbèi	~备	V:	to prepare, plan
zhúnxǔ	~许	V/N:	to permit; permission

zìdiǎn	字典	N:	dictionary
zì	自	•N:	self
zìcóng	～从	CV:	from the time of
zìshā	～杀	V:	to commit suicide
zìyóu	～由	N:	liberty
zōngjiào	宗教	N:	religion
zǒngqǐlai	总起来	RV:	to sum up
(dà) zǒngtǒng		N:	president
zū	租	V:	to rent
zūgěi	～给	V:	to rent to, lease to
zūjiè	～界	N:	concession, leased territory
zūyín	～银	N:	rental
zú	族	M:	tribe
zǔài	阻碍	V/N:	obstruct; hindrance
zǔfù	祖父	N:	father's father, grandfather
zǔxiān	～先	N:	ancestor
zuì-huì-guó	最惠国	N:	most favored nation
zūnshǒu	遵守	V:	to obey, observe
zūn(shǒu) mìng(lìng)		VO:	to obey an order
zūnzhòng	遵重	V:	to respect
zuǒyòu	左右	N:	approximately (lit: left or right)
zuò guānzhǎng		VO:	to be a top official
zuòwéi	作为	V:	treat as, to fill the function of

CPSIA information can be obtained at www.ICGtesting.com
Printed in the USA
241364LV00002B/181/P